Palgrave Studies in Economic History

Series Editor
Kent Deng, London School of Economics, London, UK

Palgrave Studies in Economic History is designed to illuminate and enrich our understanding of economies and economic phenomena of the past. The series covers a vast range of topics including financial history, labour history, development economics, commercialisation, urbanisation, industrialisation, modernisation, globalisation, and changes in world economic orders.

More information about this series at
https://link.springer.com/bookseries/14632

Robin Pearson

Delusions of Competence

The Near-Death of Lloyd's of London 1970–2002

palgrave
macmillan

Robin Pearson
Business School
University of Hull
Hull, UK

ISSN 2662-6497 ISSN 2662-6500 (electronic)
Palgrave Studies in Economic History
ISBN 978-3-030-94087-4 ISBN 978-3-030-94088-1 (eBook)
https://doi.org/10.1007/978-3-030-94088-1

Cover credit: © Melisa Hasan

This Palgrave Macmillan imprint is published by the registered company Springer Nature Switzerland AG
The registered company address is: Gewerbestrasse 11, 6330 Cham, Switzerland

Acknowledgements

Aspects of the research contained in this book were presented to the Economic History Society Annual Conference, Belfast, and to workshops at the Universities of Leeds and Durham and the Max Planck Institute for Social Research, Cologne. I am most grateful to the participants for their helpful comments, as well as to the anonymous reviewers for *Business History Review* and Palgrave Macmillan who made valuable suggestions. I also wish to thank Lloyd's of London for permission to consult their internal records, and the University of Hull for awarding me the sabbatical leave during which this book was largely completed.

CONTENTS

Abbreviations

AUA3	Additional Underwriting Agencies Ltd. 3
BL	British Library
BPR	Bellew, Parry & Raven (Broking, Underwriting and Managing Agency Group)
DTI	Department of Trade and Industry (UK)
E&O	Errors and Omissions Insurance
FCA	Financial Conduct Authority (UK)
FSA	Financial Services Authority (UK)
GW	Gooda Walker managing Agency
ILU	Institute of London Underwriters
LMX	London Market Excess of Loss Reinsurance
NA	National Archives (UK)
PWS	Pearson Webb Springbett (Brokers)
RBUA	Richard Beckett Underwriting Agencies Ltd.
RITC	Reinsurance to Close
SEC	Securities and Exchange Commission (US)
XL	Excess of Loss Reinsurance

List of Figures

CHAPTER 1

Introduction

Abstract Hitherto, explanations of the crisis at the Lloyd's insurance market in the late twentieth century have focused on the effects of catastrophic losses and poor governance. In contrast, this book argues that multiple delusions of competence were also at work. This chapter introduces this argument, evaluates the sources used, provides a definition of competence and surveys the literature on professional and scientific expertise, and the related research on behavioural economics and cognitive psychology. This literature has uncovered some of the fundamental behavioural responses that underpin notions of competence and that influence decision making under uncertainty. These findings can help us better understand why the crisis at Lloyd's took the disastrous course that it did.

Keyword Lloyd's of London · Insurance · Expertise · Competence · Decision making under uncertainty

Rapid structural change resulting from the collapse of an economic system is a less common phenomenon in insurance than in the history of other financial institutions, such as banks and stock markets, where flows of capital and credit act as highly visible indicators of market confidence

R. Pearson, *Delusions of Competence*,
Palgrave Studies in Economic History,
https://doi.org/10.1007/978-3-030-94088-1_1

and volatility.[1] Catastrophic losses, of course, have periodically delivered shocks to the insurance industry. The San Francisco earthquake and fire of 1906, for instance, led to an influx of European reinsurance companies into the US and the exit of weaker American and foreign direct insurance companies.[2] In this and other similar cases, however, such catastrophes largely resulted in the rearrangement of players on the field, rather than a fundamental change in industry structures or practices.[3]

One exception to this general pattern was the late twentieth-century crisis that afflicted one of the world's oldest and most famous insurance institutions, Lloyd's of London. Hitherto, explanations of the crisis have focused on the frauds, catastrophic losses and issues of inadequate governance that plagued Lloyd's from the late 1970s to the early 1990s. Such accounts, notwithstanding their excellence, were written, mostly contemporaneously, either by journalists seeking to tell an exciting story of City scandals, or by Lloyd's insiders, some of whom had witnessed their investments being wiped out, and who sought to blame those who governed Lloyd's during this period.[4]

This book represents the first scholarly study of the crisis written from an historical perspective. In contrast to previous accounts, it argues that the above factors—fraud, external catastrophes and poor governance—while important, were not sufficient. Together, these may not have resulted in the near death of Lloyd's had many of the actors involved not also suffered from multiple delusions of competence. Arrogance, elitism, greed, corruption and stubborn resistance to reform in defence

[1] An economic system may be defined for present purposes as the process of organising and allocating resources and inputs to produce outputs such as products or services.

[2] Direct insurance is where an insurer sells insurance protection to a customer. Reinsurance is the device by which a direct insurer (re-)insures with another insurer part of a risk that he/she has first insured; that is, it is the insurance of insurers.

[3] On the insurance market before and after the San Francisco fire, see Pearson and Lönnborg, 'Naturkatastrofer'; Röder, *Rechtsbildung*; Trebilcock, *Phoenix Assurance*. On the longevity of modern underwriting practices in reinsurance, see Jarzabkowski et. al., *Making a Market*.

[4] Hodgson, *Lloyd's of London*; Mantle, *For Whom the Bell Tolls*; Gunn, *Nightmare on Lime Street*; Raphael, *Ultimate Risk*; Luessenhop, *Risky Business*; Proctor, *For Whom the Bell Tolls*; Duguid, *On the Brink*. The impact on direct insurers of the liability reinsurance crisis, and of Lloyd's financial distress, has been examined respectively by Berger et. al., "Reinsurance", and Fields et. al., "Lloyd's Financial Distress". Neither discuss the situation at Lloyd's at any length.

of vested interests comprised endogenous elements of the crisis, which compounded the series of exogenous shocks to insurance operations. Politically entrenched ideas about the virtues of self-regulation, and an exaggerated faith in the ability of insider experts to know what was best, also played a role. The result was a belated misdiagnosis of what ailed Lloyd's and a series of institutional reforms that, while targeting the visible symptoms of the disease, failed to cure its underlying causes.

The issue of competence, which may be defined as 'a sufficiency of qualification' or 'a capacity to deal adequately with a subject', relates directly to the question of trust in experts and their expertise.[5] Political debates currently swirl around this issue with ever fiercer velocity. Recent controversies have particularly focused on the influence of medical experts, epidemiologists and environmental scientists in shaping the policies of governments towards the Covid-19 pandemic and climate change.[6] The nature, quality and accuracy of, and trust in, experts and their decisions, however, have also been widely discussed in a wide range of other areas, including surgery, health care, veterinary medicine, the wine and food industry, nuclear power, disaster recovery, education, art criticism, financial forecasting, construction, workplace safety, the energy industry, forestry, agriculture, transportation, public procurement, crime, forensic science and expert testimony before courts of law.[7]

This large body of literature on professional and scientific expertise has been closely allied to the pioneering research conducted in behavioural economics and cognitive psychology over recent decades. This research has uncovered some of the fundamental behavioural responses that underpin notions of competence, and that influence decision making, especially under conditions of uncertainty and imperfect information. These findings, which can only be summarised here, can help us better

[5] This rudimentary definition is from the *Oxford English Dictionary*, but it is broad enough to encompass the functional, cognitive and behavioural abilities that comprise a holistic and multi-dimensional definition of competence. Cf. Deist and Winterton, 'What is Competence'.

[6] For example: Battiston et.al., 'Reliance on Scientists'; O'Shea and Ueda, 'Experts' Advice'; Bylund and Packard, 'Separation of Power'; Webb, 'Enough of Experts?'.

[7] Examples include: Clarke and Knights, 'Practice makes Perfect?'; Currie and Macleod, 'Diagnosing Expertise'; Lidén and Dror, 'Expert Reliability'; Garrett and Mitchell, 'Proficiency of Experts'.

understand why the crisis at Lloyd's took the disastrous course that it did.

It is now generally accepted that decision making in fast-moving environments is associated with, and facilitated by, intuition and a reliance on the heuristic or rule of thumb.[8] As experimental psychologists have shown, however, intuitive decision making also generates systematic biases and errors in predictions. In particular, people tend to judge a risk based on the ease with which instances of it come to mind. They also often ignore the effects of random variation in small samples and wrongly apply the law of large numbers to them.[9] The success of intuitive decision making depends greatly on the predictability of the environment in which decisions are made.[10] Intuition, however, can lead decision-makers, when confronted with a difficult problem, to simplify the decision, rather than applying a more sophisticated decision rule based on fuller information.[11]

Intuitive thinking has been shown to be closely related to perceptions of expertise. Visual cues, for example, facial expressions, body language and clothing, can quickly dominate people's judgements of competence and performance. Research has found that such judgements are highly correlated with the perceived attractiveness, dominance, maturity, masculinity and status of an individual, as well as with racial and gender stereotypes.[12] When it comes to judging one's own competence, individuals are prone to egocentric biases, such as overconfidence and the illusion of control.[13] In stable environments, 'where an individual expects to continue a large proportion of his current activities and relationships for a long time in the future', overconfidence can be costly when it leads to complacency and low levels of innovation.[14] Some scholars have called

[8] Kahneman, *Thinking Fast and Slow*.

[9] *Ibid*., 7, 112–113; Yuan, 'Lure of Illusory Luck'.

[10] Kahneman, *Thinking Fast and Slow*, 201, 240.

[11] *Ibid*., 237, 243; Hey et.al., 'Theories of Decision Making'.

[12] Tolsá-Caballero and Tsay, 'Blinded by our Sight'.

[13] Fellner et al., 'Illusion of Expertise'.

[14] Dessi and Zhao, 'Overconfidence'; Malmendier and Tate, 'CEO Overconfidence'. Not all scholars agree that overconfidence is costly. Berg and Lein, 'Investor Overconfidence', argue that overconfidence among uninformed securities traders about experts' predictive ability and the quality of their information can lead to increased trading, improved liquidity and lower transaction costs.

this the 'curse of expertise': namely the way that an individual's professional or market experience, and his/her self-perception of competence, can produce 'cognitive dissonance', in other words a reduced willingness and ability to pay heed to the perspectives of others and a failure to take into account information, for example about a risk event, that lies outside the bounds of his/her own knowledge.[15] In short, experts systematically demonstrate an inability to know the limits of their expertise, and people in general systematically fail to recognise their own incompetence. Overconfidence can lead individuals to suffer from an optimistic bias in their predictions and to persist in operating according to established beliefs. Associated with this are several other observed phenomena: 'tunnelling', namely the instinct to make inferences too quickly and to focus on a small number of known sources of uncertainty; convergent behaviour within a group and 'herding', namely the desire to avoid being an outlier in one's predictions, which has been widely observed of professional economists and financial forecasters; and 'confirmation bias', whereby experts try to interpret evidence with the aim of corroborating the rules that they had already made up.[16] The following account of Lloyd's applies some of these behavioural insights. We also return to them in the concluding discussion.

A wide range of sources have been consulted for this book: parliamentary papers and debates; contemporary newspapers; UK government records; Lloyd's Corporation internal records, including annual reports, the *Lloyd's Log* in-house magazine, and records of Council and Committee meetings and general meetings of members; and interviews recorded with Lloyd's officers, brokers and underwriters. As always with any historical investigation, the bias of evidence must be considered. Lloyd's records, even those not intended for outside consumption, were carefully presented, apparently with the effect of minimising the appearance of conflict within the governing bodies, namely the Committee of

[15] Zhang et al., 'Errors of Experts'; Fisher and Keil, 'Curse of Expertise'; Kang and Sim, 'Fragility of Experts'.

[16] Taleb, *Black Swan*, 58, 61, 149–51; Angner, 'Economists as Experts'; Ashiya and Doi, 'Herd Behavior'; Bewley and Fiebig, 'Interest Rate Forecasters'; Kang and Kim, 'Fragility of Experts'; Banerjee, 'Simple Model'; Deaves et. al., 'Dynamics of Overconfidence'; Dunning et. al, 'Why People Fail'; Bikhchandani et. al., 'Learning'; Acemoglu et.al., 'Bayesian Learning'.

Lloyd's to 1982, and, from 1983, the Council of Lloyd's and its sub-committees. It is rare to read in these records any criticism, overt or implicit, of the Chairman of Council, and even the resignation of the Chief Executive Officer in November 1985 was passed over without comment, despite the acrimony that it caused. As a result, it is necessary always to read between the lines or to watch for telling phrases that may allude to dissent or contrary views. Lloyd's entered the 1980s regarding itself as essentially a private society, and nervous about revealing its inner workings to outsiders, while at the same time always keen to present itself as a jewel in the crown of UK financial services.

It has also been necessary to consider the agendas of parties outside Lloyd's who took part in debates about reforming the institution—most obviously the political ideologies of individual MPs, and the personal vested interests of many of them as members of Lloyd's—as well as the desire of journalists to sensationalise stories or stretch evidence to fit their chosen narratives. To an extent, caution must also be applied to the evidence of disgruntled Lloyd's members campaigning for redress through law suits or the website truthaboutlloyds.com, or through the books and articles that they authored about the crisis.

Finally, watchfulness is also necessary with regard to the self-delusions of individual actors. One interesting example of this is Sir Peter Miller, chairman of Lloyd's in the mid-1980s, who in a 1989 interview declared himself to be 'anti-Establishment', which he defined as someone who dislikes being told what to do by persons in authority. Miller may have been 'bloody minded'—his own words—like many of the Lloyd's underwriters whom he admired, but with his deeply conservative political views and his social and educational background—he was schooled at Rugby and Oxford, his parents were barristers, his grandfather was a shipowner and banker, he could not be described as anti-Establishment in any sense.[17] Self-evaluations must be regarded with suspicion.

The following chapter provides a brief overview of the history of Lloyd's and the ways in which the market was organised between the eighteenth and mid-twentieth centuries. Chapter 3 provides an analysis of the social composition of Lloyd's and the political and economic outlook of its working members and leaders. Chapter 4 describes the scandals of the 1970s and early 1980s and the institutional and public response to

[17] BL C409/015, interview with Sir Peter Miller.

these. Chapter 5 examines the first phase of reforms commencing with the new Lloyd's Act of 1982. Chapters 6 and 7 provide, respectively, accounts of the major scandals that dogged Lloyd's through the 1980s, and the liability crisis and LMX spiral that nearly brought down Lloyd's by the mid-1990s. Chapter 8 describes the subsequent reforms that enabled Lloyd's to survive, albeit in an entirely restructured form. The conclusion points to the implications of this history for the role of financial service regulation and to the dangers for complex financial systems of entrenched beliefs in the competence of experts and the efficacy of self-governance. An epilogue provides a brief overview of developments during the last two decades and offers a retrospective view on the differences between Lloyd's now and as it was just 40 years ago.

CHAPTER 2

Lloyd's: Its History and Business Practices

Abstract From the 1680s, customers of Edward Lloyd's coffee house in the City of London began transacting marine insurance for England's growing seaborne trade. Initially, they wrote insurance on their own behalf, each assuming part of the risk of a ship's hull or cargo on any given voyage. During the following centuries, Lloyd's underwriters associated together as a society, but continued to write insurance on an individual basis with unlimited personal liability. As risk values rose with technological and economic development, individuals began to group in syndicates, with some actively underwriting on behalf of the non-working members of their syndicate. Lloyd's diversified into other areas, such as motor and aviation insurance. Underwriting and broking functions also separated, and large broking firms began to acquire control over syndicates. The latter development gave rise to conflicts of interest that eventually helped to undermine the traditional organisation of Lloyd's.

Keyword Lloyd's of London · Underwriters · Syndicates · Brokers · Unlimited liability

R. Pearson, *Delusions of Competence*,
Palgrave Studies in Economic History,
https://doi.org/10.1007/978-3-030-94088-1_2

During the 1680s, customers of Edward Lloyd's coffee house in the City of London began to transact marine insurance for England's growing seaborne trade.[1] In 1720, the underwriters working out of Lloyd's were joined in the marine insurance market by two new chartered companies, the Royal Exchange Assurance and the London Assurance, who were granted a monopoly of underwriting of ships and cargoes on a corporate basis. For the next century, the individual underwriters at Lloyd's co-existed with these two London insurance corporations, though the latter, owing to their higher costs and more conservative approach to underwriting, never acquired more than five per cent of the UK marine insurance market.

From 1734, the coffee house published *Lloyd's List,* which provided shipping intelligence to those who subscribed to the paper. The first formal organisation was the 'Society of Underwriters', who in 1760 established *Lloyd's Register of Shipping*, also on a subscription basis. Nine years later, concerned by the increasing number of gamblers and speculators in the market, a group of underwriters left to form a New Lloyd's and to publish an improved version of *Lloyd's List*. By 1774, the New Lloyd's had 179 subscriber-members frequenting their premises in the Royal Exchange. This soon replaced the previous incarnation of Lloyd's.

With the rapid expansion of demand for marine insurance during Britain's wars against France at the end of the eighteenth century, the membership of Lloyd's temporarily soared to over 2,000. This growth attracted would-be promoters of new insurance companies, who attacked the two London corporations for their monopoly privileges, and Lloyd's underwriters for the alleged inadequacy of their funds. The response of Lloyd's was to formalise the organisation of their market. In 1811, a deed of association was drawn up, a new governing committee established, and the first agents appointed. The latter were tasked with transmitting shipping intelligence, overseeing salvage operations and ship repairs, and adjusting claims. By 1820, there were over 250 Lloyd's agents located at ports in the UK and abroad.

Following the repeal of the two chartered monopolies in 1824, new marine insurance companies began to be formed. These gradually made inroads into Lloyd's business. By the 1870s, there were several dozen marine insurance companies in the UK, who together accounted for some

[1] The following paragraphs are based on Wright and Fayle, *History of Lloyd's*; Kingston, 'Marine Insurance'; Pearson, 'Lloyd's of London'.

40% of the market. The challenging economic conditions of the 1870s and 1880s, with a slow-down in international trade, lower premium rates for steamships and competition from companies that often pooled information and standardised practices through their trade associations, made life tougher for the underwriters at Lloyd's.

Lloyd's responded, again successfully, by embracing regulatory and organisational change, by adjusting risk assessment to new shipping technologies and by product diversification. Novel lines of insurance such as burglary, trade credit, earthquake, hurricane, motor and aviation insurance were pioneered by leading underwriters, notably Cuthbert Heath. In 1871, Lloyd's became incorporated as a society by act of Parliament.[2] This gave Lloyd's a constitution, which set out the voting rights of members and procedures for general meetings and the election of the committee, and provided the latter with the power to make by-laws and appoint officers. The incorporating act remained the principal legislation governing Lloyd's for the next 100 years.[3] It was intended to strengthen the committee's rule-making powers. It did not remove the unlimited personal liability of members for insurance losses, nor did it impose any legal liability on the Society to cover the unpaid losses of insolvent members. From the 1850s, guarantees or deposits to help safeguard against underwriting failures had been sometimes required of members, but they became mandatory in 1882. In 1908, Cuthbert Heath introduced mandatory certificates of solvency for the members of his syndicates. This was called, rather inaccurately, an annual audit, though it was actually a test of whether or not the assets of each member were sufficient to meet his underwriting liabilities, rather than an examination of the accuracy of his accounts.[4] The 'annual audit' was adopted by a general meeting of Lloyd's members that same year, and a central trust

[2] 34 Vict. (1871) c. 21.

[3] Subsequent (private) amending acts merely extended Lloyd's powers to make its own byelaws, and (in 1911) belatedly removed the 1871 clause that confined the business of Lloyd's to marine insurance. 1 & 2 Geo. V (1911) c. 62; 15 & 16 Geo. V (1925) c. 26.

[4] Wright and Fayle *History of Lloyd's*, 424–5. Ian Hay Davison stated that solvency certificates 'were not audits by any normal definition...Once obligations were covered, the auditor stopped counting'. Davison, *Lloyd's*, 110.

fund was also established into which all premiums were to be paid, to be used to cover any outstanding claims on members who became insolvent.[5]

The 1871 act also specified the division between underwriting and non-underwriting members that characterised the market throughout the following century and gave rise to the conflicts that so exercised the reformers of the 1980s. Only underwriting members were to be permitted to write insurance at Lloyd's and use the Lloyd's standard policy form, all underwriting had to be carried out on the floor of Lloyd's, named 'the Room', and underwriters could only deal with other members.

By the early twentieth century, these non-active subscriber-members had become known as 'Names', that is individuals who put up their personal wealth as capital, but who did not actively underwrite themselves.[6] They were organised into syndicates in which insured risks were pooled by the syndicate's underwriter. A Name's declared means determined how much could be insured on his behalf—women were not admitted as Names until 1970. Solvency was, in theory, ensured by limiting the underwriting capacity of a syndicate to the assets of its members, but there continued to be no legal limit to their individual liability.

Lloyd's syndicates were not legal partnerships. At the end of every year, each syndicate was formally disbanded as a trading entity, but then usually reconstituted for the following year, often with the same membership and the same identifying number. Because claims arising from ocean-going voyages could take time to be reported and settled, the practice developed of waiting three years from the beginning of a syndicate before 'closing' one year's account and declaring a profit or loss.[7] This three-year accounting system thus commenced with year one's premium income and allowed two further years for claims to come in before the result for year one was declared. The result also included setting aside reserves for

[5] Partly as a result of these reforms, the Assurance Companies Act of 1909 left Lloyd's untouched, with the corporation retaining full responsibility for regulating the activities of its members.

[6] I have been unable to find out exactly when the term 'Name' was first coined. The trust deed of 1811 refers only to 'subscribers'. The acts of 1871 and 1911 refer to 'members'. It may have been the early twentieth century when 'Name' was first generally used, as it is in this paper, to refer to all members of Lloyd's, both active underwriters and 'passive' non-underwriting members.

[7] This also became the standard practice of the new marine insurance companies of the nineteenth century, both in the UK and elsewhere.

future claims that had not yet come in during the three-year period. How much to set aside was difficult to estimate. In the twentieth century, some types of 'long-tail' non-marine liability insurance produced claims that arrived decades after the policies were written. The reserve was normally set aside by buying a reinsurance policy that would pay for any future claims. This was known as 'reinsurance-to-close' (RITC).[8] The reinsurer was often another Lloyd's syndicate, sometimes the immediate successor of the syndicate paying for the RITC. Thus, a Name joining a syndicate with a long history of such transactions might pick up the personal unlimited liability for losses on policies written a long time before. This was a key feature of the crisis that unfolded in the 1980s.

Although Lloyd's was incorporated in 1871, it was not a company with capital, shareholders, directors or any mutual pooling of risks across syndicates. Rather, it was a society of individual members—Lloyd's insiders often also referred to it as a 'community'—who, organised into syndicates, wrote insurance on their own behalf in a market whose broad rules of conduct and entry were set by the governing committee.

Between the late 1940s and 1960, the exports of North America, Western Europe and Japan more than doubled. With the post-war revival in global trade, UK marine insurance expanded rapidly. In 1947, the marine tariffs that had given some protection to companies were abolished. This resulted in an increasing volume of business being brought to Lloyd's. By 1956, Lloyd's accounted for over 60% of all marine insurance transacted in the UK and a similar share of the smaller market in aviation insurance.[9] As the Lloyd's market expanded and became better regulated, its membership grew. There were 476 underwriting members of Lloyd's in 1883, but 1,532 by 1933. Membership further rose to 3,157 by 1952 and then doubled again to over 6,000 by the late 1960s.[10] One marine underwriter, who commenced working there in 1942, recalled the 'hurry hurry bustle bustle' atmosphere of the 1950s.[11] The growth of business required more capacious accommodation. The original underwriting room in the Royal Exchange was abandoned in 1928 and Lloyd's

[8] For an overview of RITC, see Rice and White, 'Reinsurance to Close'.

[9] *The Review*, 15 November 1957.

[10] Membership figures from Raynes, *History of British Insurance*, 318; Cockerell, 'Lloyd's of London', 280.

[11] BL C409/027, interview with Terence Higgins.

moved into a new building at 12 Leadenhall Street. Thirty years later, another new building was constructed in Lime Street.

Notwithstanding the ebb and flow of the underwriting cycle, the first two-thirds of the twentieth century were generally profitable for Lloyd's. One Lloyd's man declared to the journalist Paul Ferris in 1960:

> My dear chap… there's no business in my experience where such an agreeable income can be earned in such agreeable surroundings with a minimum of output. It's a golden business.[12]

As they had in previous centuries, Lloyd's underwriters proved more flexible than their counterparts in the insurance companies and more willing to accept large, unusual or novel risks. By selective underwriting and keeping administrative costs low, they were also able to undercut the rates charged by the companies. Beginning in the inter-war years, then accelerating in the decades after the Second World War, motor insurance was one major driver of growth. There were 3.4m vehicles on UK roads in 1950. By 1984, there were 20.8m. Collisions increased while inflation drove up the cost of repairs.[13] From 1965, Lloyd's allowed its motor syndicates to deal directly with non-Lloyd's intermediaries, provided the latter were sponsored by a broker who was a member of Lloyd's. Another growth area was transatlantic reinsurance. Reinsurance business, including the American offshore oil industry and much aviation insurance, gravitated to London for its specialist services and its willingness to underwrite very large risks.[14] By the mid-1960s, about half of Lloyd's business was derived from the United States, where Lloyd's reputation for 'absolute reliability…decency and fairness…(and) a spirit of inventiveness…' was growing.[15] The historian Welf Werner has shown that Lloyd's and the rest of the London market accepted ever larger quantities of US reinsurances up to the calamity of Hurricane Betsy in August 1965, and profited

[12] Ferris, *The City*, 193.

[13] Trebilcock, *Phoenix Assurance*, 953.

[14] On the growth of the 'London market', which, as well as Lloyd's, included UK companies, and foreign companies selling reinsurance through UK-based brokers, see Pearson, 'United Kingdom'.

[15] Daenzer, 'Non-Admitted Market', 36.

greatly by retroceding the most hazardous parts of these American risks back to weakly competitive American reinsurers.[16]

As individual risks and the overall volume of business became larger, and the market further diversified into new lines of insurance, the average size of members' syndicates increased. In the 1880s, few syndicates had more than six names. By the 1980s, some had several thousand. As syndicates became larger, they became administered by managing agents, who appointed the active underwriters, canvassed for Names, oversaw the syndicate's activities and received a fee plus a commission on the syndicate's profits. Managing agents often ran more than one syndicate. During the 1970s, Names' or members' agents also emerged. These recruited Names to syndicates in return for an annual fee assessed on the 'stamp' (underwriting) capacity of their Names.[17]

Outsiders seeking insurance could not do business directly with Lloyd's. They were required to hire brokers registered by Lloyd's. Equally, a rule stipulating that underwriting at Lloyd's could only be conducted with other members ensured that brokers who wished to place business at Lloyd's had also to become members. Underwriters' 'boxes', the equivalent of traders' market stalls, were grouped around the Room according to the line of insurance that the underwriter specialised in—marine, non-marine, aviation, motor, etc. Brokers seeking insurance for a ship or a cargo would usually start by visiting the box of the principle or 'lead' marine underwriter known as a specialist in the particular type of risk that required insurance.[18] Up to the 1980s at least, bowler hats might still be doffed, pleasantries exchanged, and the bargaining over prices and terms would commence. If the underwriter liked the risk, he might offer to insure part of it at a given premium rate. In this case, the broker would have to then go around the boxes of other marine underwriters in the Room, and sometimes also to insurance companies outside Lloyd's, in order to buy further insurance to complete the cover

[16] Werner, 'Hurricane Betsy'. Retrocession is the device by which a reinsurer insures with another insurer part of the risk that she has reinsured; that is, it is the insurance of reinsurers.

[17] Luessenhop, *Risky Business*, 72, 108, 127.

[18] The following account of traditional underwriting in the Room is based on BL C409/027, interview with Terence Higgins; Brown, *Hazard Unlimited*, 12–13. The negotiating process itself had many similarities with that still used recently by reinsurance companies, as described by Jarzubowksi et. al., *Making a Market*.

required. If the 'lead' underwriter had stated a rate and policy conditions for the insurance, most often the rate and conditions would be closely followed by other underwriters in the Room, in a form of acknowledgement of the expertise of the lead. This process at Lloyd's of negotiating over premium rates displayed many of the classic features of 'herding' behaviour that, as noted in the previous chapter, scholars have found among other professional groups.

Brokers and underwriters often came to know each other well—the underwriters' box was a small, intimate space. The personal history of deals between the parties, and trust and reputation, was important in determining whether or not an insurance would be made. Brokers, however, would never allow underwriters to meet their clients. Consequently, underwriters would seldom see the ships or other risks that they were insuring, yet they were supposed to profess a considerable knowledge about them. The underwriter might examine what had previously been charged on risks of the same type, and there were printed aides to which they had access, such as *Lloyd's Register* and the *Confidential Index* (a listing of all ships and their sizes owned by shipowners). The information in these manuals would be consulted, usually with the broker present, before the underwriter decided whether or not to write a risk. As successful underwriters became more experienced, some claimed that they developed a 'sixth sense', an intuition, about whether a risk was right or not.

Before the First World War, there had been no formal separation between underwriters and brokers. The latter were often family firms or small partnerships that combined overseas commodity trading and shipping agencies with some broking or underwriting of marine insurance.[19] Towards the end of the nineteenth century, however, some of these firms grew to become limited companies, placing risks with those syndicates of Lloyd's members or external insurance companies that they came to control. The broking firms also increasingly consolidated their business through mergers, which provided a means of securing a succession in the event of a failure of the founding families to acquire leadership continuity or specialist underwriting skills. Such mergers led to a rising concentration of market share, a trend that accelerated after the Second

[19] One example is the Hogg Robinson group, which commenced in 1845 as a partnership between a wine merchant and an insurance broker-cum-merchant. Chapman, 'Hogg Robinson'.

World War. By 1978, 68% of premiums at Lloyd's were placed by the dozen leading broking firms. Lloyd's became particularly attractive to US broking companies seeking a foothold in London market. Even the largest Lloyd's brokers found themselves vulnerable to takeover by their American counterparts.[20]

Most managing agencies became owned by a handful of these giant broking firms. Through the agencies, the brokers controlled most of the syndicates and therefore indirectly employed most of the underwriters. The potential thus arose for a conflict of interest between brokers who sought the lowest rates for their clients and underwriters who sought the best risks at the highest rates for their Names. This fundamental flaw in its organisational structure was just one of several pressure points that brought the Lloyd's market to the brink of destruction towards the end of the twentieth century.

[20] For examples, see *The Times* 23 January, 20 December 1980.

CHAPTER 3

Lloyd's People: Their Social Composition and Political Economy

Abstract There was a strange duality about Lloyd's in the twentieth century. On the one hand, it demonstrated an impressive capacity for product innovation and underwriting flexibility. On the other hand, Lloyd's was also widely regarded as an elitist old boys' club with arcane rules and opaque practices. An analysis of the social composition of Lloyd's, and the political and economic outlook of its working members and leaders, reveals its hierarchical and highly conservative character. There was a tradition of informal learning on the job and a disdain for formal education that proved hard to change. It was believed that competence should not be subject to external regulation or monitoring, but should only be assessed by the practitioners themselves. Self-regulation, freedom of trade and non-interference in the independence of underwriters and brokers were the core principles of Lloyd's and defended to the hilt.

Keyword Lloyd's of London · Financial innovation · Public schools · Social elites · Self-regulation

R. Pearson, *Delusions of Competence*, Palgrave Studies in Economic History, https://doi.org/10.1007/978-3-030-94088-1_3

There was a strange duality about Lloyd's in the twentieth century. On the one hand, it demonstrated an impressive capacity for product innovation and flexibility by diversifying into new lines such as burglary, engineering, motor, aviation, trade credit and various kinds of liability and indemnity insurance.[1] Later, it extended to insure oil tankers, oil rigs, satellites, natural disasters, and large, idiosyncratic or hard-to-place risks.[2] A major growth area was US property and casualty reinsurance, which by the 1960s accounted for about half of Lloyd's business.[3] Lloyd's was widely lauded in government and economic circles as an institution of global repute that played a vital role in the UK economy. A general meeting of members in 1976 was told that Lloyd's contributed 60% of all earnings from overseas insurance and almost eight per cent of the UK's net overseas invisible earnings in the private sector. 'This achievement rests not least on the maintenance of Lloyd's reputation throughout the world as an international insurance market and on its ability to react quickly and flexibly to the rapidly changing conditions of world trade'.[4] The Corporation was a regular stop on any tour organised by the UK Foreign and Commonwealth Office for foreign dignitaries, as well as being regularly visited by government ministers, public figures and members of the British royal family. In the year to May 1976, for instance, VIPs included Princess Anne, the Aga Khan, the President of Gambia, nine ambassadors, five high commissioners, the Vice-President of the EEC Commission, the leader of the UK parliamentary opposition, the Shadow Chancellor, the Home Secretary and the US senator Hubert Humphrey.[5] Distinguished visitors in the following year included the Archbishop of Canterbury, the Secretary of State for Trade, the President of Kuwait, the President of the European Commission, 11 ambassadors and the High Commissioner of New Zealand.[6] The Prince of Wales paid

[1] Brown, *Cuthbert Heath*; Pearson, 'Cuthbert Eden Heath'.

[2] An example of the latter was actress Elizabeth Taylor's Cartier diamond, insured for $1.2m at a premium of $66,000, on condition that it was taken out of its vault for no more than 30 days in any one year and under armed guard. *The Times* 2 January 1970.

[3] Werner, 'Hurricane Betsy'.

[4] Report of the Committee of Lloyd's 1975–1976, in Lloyd's, *Minutes of the General Meeting*.

[5] *Ibid.*, 13.

[6] Report of the Committee of Lloyd's 1976–1977, in Lloyd's, *Minutes of the General Meeting*, 12.

an 'informal educational' visit in 1979, and in the same year, his grandmother opened Lloyd's new administration building at Chatham.[7] Queen Elizabeth the Queen Mother was arguably Lloyd's favourite royal. She also opened Lloyd's new building at One Lime Street in 1986.[8]

On the other hand, even while presenting this face of a successful financial institution to the outside world, Lloyd's was also widely regarded as an elitist old boys' club with arcane rules and opaque practices.[9] Those who worked at Lloyd's between the 1940s and 1970s recalled an 'all-male society' with a highly defined hierarchy.[10] At the top were the senior brokers and chief underwriters, the latter often described as 'god-like' figures who ruled over their small staffs of deputy underwriters and clerks. At the bottom were the employees of Lloyd's Corporation, including liveried doormen and porters still quaintly referred to as 'waiters' in a nod to the origins of Lloyd's as a coffee house. These were 'very much kind of servants' from lower middle-class backgrounds, some of whom spent their entire working lives at Lloyd's.[11]

There were two main types of men who worked in the Room. Sir Peter Miller referred disparagingly to the first type:

> There were an awful lot in those days of the gilded lilies in Lloyd's, as I used to call them. Remember, 'they toil not neither do they spin', and they swanned around Lloyd's, having been made members of Lloyd's by their proud families, because they really weren't intelligent enough to do anything else.[12]

[7] Notes of Proceedings at a General Meeting, 7 November 1979, in Lloyd's, *Minutes of the General Meeting*, 11; Lloyd's, *Annual Report for 1979*. Prince Charles was back at Lloyd's ten years later for lunch. Council meeting 11 January 1989, in Lloyd's, *Minutes of Council, no.5*.

[8] See *Lloyd's Log*, Royal issue, November 1986.

[9] Some syndicates in the early 1970s still insisted on writing with quills. Anthony Brown, *Hazard Unlimited*, 10. A leading non-marine underwriter, who had worked in Lloyd's since 1939, described it as a 'business club' whose members had few contacts elsewhere in the City. BL C409/026, interview with Leonard Toomey.

[10] BL C409/027, interview with Terence Higgins.

[11] BL C409/020, interview with Dennis Presland; C409/067, interview with Francis Holford.

[12] BL C409/015, interview with Sir Peter Miller. Miller was referring to Christ's counsel to his disciples in *Matthew* 6, v. 28: 'Consider the lilies of the field, how they grow; they neither toil nor spin...'.

Bertie Hiscox, a future deputy chairman, found Lloyd's in the 1960s frequented by 'the thick pin-striped boy made a member by his daddy… I thought I'd come to a place for the mentally disabled'.[13] The second type were those whom Miller called the 'determined' men, mostly from a comfortable, but not 'gilded', professional or commercial background. Miller, who began working at Lloyd's for his family's broking business in 1954, recalled: 'There were an awful lot of people in Lloyd's of my type, who had their way to make, and were determined to do so'.[14] The thing that both types had in common was a public school (i.e. private) education, with the first group likely to enter Lloyd's directly from school, and the second group more likely to do so after having attended Oxford or Cambridge. In a sample of 36 Lloyd's Council members between 1985 and 1991, we have details on the secondary schooling of 29.[15] All but three of these had attended a public school, often as boarders, including four who went to Eton. Of the 17 whose university details are known, 14 attended Oxbridge. Thirteen of the 35 also had some sort of military experience, often having done National Service in the 1950s. There were common features too in the residence and recreational activities of Lloyd's underwriters and brokers. Many had family homes either in London or in the rural home counties, especially Kent, Surrey, Sussex—or in both. The most popular recreations were the country pursuits of shooting, fishing and hunting, together with music and opera, closely followed by skiing, sailing and golf. In short, these wealthy people shared leisure activities that were, unsurprisingly, characteristic of their social class.

This common background, anchored in the English public school, determined the culture and modes of thought of those who led Lloyd's between the 1940s and 1980s. Recent accounts have argued that public schools provided an education in exclusivity, racism, sexism, patriotism, the greatness of the British Empire, ambition, the importance of class differences as bedrock of the British social order and a keen sense

[13] Cited by Luessenhop, *Risky Business*, 100.

[14] BL C409/015, interview with Sir Peter Miller.

[15] This sample was largely, but not entirely, based on the short biographical sketches in the series 'Lloyd's leaders' published in *Lloyd's Log* between 1985 and 1991. The sample is not fully representative of the traditional working members at Lloyd's, because it includes several outsiders, including the first two Chief Executive Officers and some non-working members elected to Council after the Neill reforms of 1987, who mostly came to Lloyd's with both a university education and external professional qualifications.

of unearned superiority and self-confidence.[16] Public schools still only educate seven per cent of pupils in England, yet they produce 74% of senior judges, 71% of senior officers in the UK armed forces, 55% of permanent secretaries in Whitehall, 50% of cabinet ministers and members of the House of Lords and 44% of captains of industry.[17] In short, Lloyd's drew its leaders, underwriters and brokers from the same social pool that supplied the core of the British governing class, and, unsurprisingly, they mirrored its outlook.

This was revealed, for example, in attitudes in the Room towards women when they were first permitted to work there in the 1970s. Women were seen by older members as an undesirable break with tradition, and by younger members largely as objects to be flirted with or harassed, though Lloyd's was hardly unique in the City in this regard. Monika Day, one of the first marine underwriters at Lloyd's, felt that the atmosphere there in the 1980s was 'Dickensian'. Still in her 20s, she moved to Lloyd's having run the marine department at General Accident plc, but spent her first day there typing.[18] The major broking firm Willis Faber pioneered the introduction of women brokers at Lloyd's in 1972. One of their divisional directors, Taravat Taher-Zadeh, recalled that there was much resistance to women in the Room when she first came to Lloyd's in 1977. Eleven years later, some of the novelty had worn off, yet there were still all-male preserves, such as brokers' dinners and clients' meetings, from which she was excluded.[19]

Before the 1970s, and possibly later than that, many if not most underwriters and brokers joined Lloyd's directly from school. There was no formal training required to work in the Room. Terence Higgins joined Lloyd's in 1942 aged 17 as a junior clerk to a marine underwriter, without any academic qualifications or relevant work experience. He obtained the job interview through a customer of his father's shirt-making business, who happened to own a small underwriting firm. Initially, his was 'a pen pushing' job, copying into ledgers, shuffling masses of paper, 'and looking, listening and learning' from the underwriter 'and getting to know people'. A companionship developed among the juniors: 'The

16 Verkaik, *Posh Boys*; Beard, *Sad Little Men*.

17 Numbers from Verkaik, *Posh Boys*, prologue.

18 BL C409/121, interview with Monika Day.

19 *Lloyd's Log*, November 1988: 41–5.

whole business was seemingly very casual and easy going'. Lloyds 'seemed to be an extension of my life at boarding school'. Higgins did start a four-year course run by the Insurance Institute of London, but gave it up after a year, having been persuaded by an older colleague that 'book learning' was 'a waste of time'.[20]

This tradition of informal learning on the job proved hard to change. During the 1970s, Lloyd's finally introduced training schemes: in 1977, some 100 courses were attended by 1,700 students from around the world, with topics ranging from a rudimentary introduction to Lloyd's to courses in management techniques for underwriting agencies and broking firms.[21] Younger staff were encouraged, but not required, to obtain qualifications awarded by the Chartered Insurance Institute, but none of these courses directly addressed the skills needed to work at an underwriter's box. A general meeting of Lloyd's was told in 1977 that 'training is largely an internal matter'.[22] A year earlier, Lloyd's Committee asserted that:

> ... it would be disastrous if the increasing pace and complexity of our business were ever to allow it to be thought that technical knowledge and ability is more important than the manner in which the business is offered and accepted; or that expediency can ever justify a lack of openness in any dealing.

Young recruits to the Room were to be guided by their senior colleagues, and they.

> should have it drummed into them from the beginning that the flexibility and lack of bureaucracy, which enables business to be done in a spirit of mutual confidence, is the cornerstone of all our operations.[23]

Despite the nod to formal education that the early training schemes represented, Lloyd's Committee retained their belief, reflecting a view widely

[20] BL C409/027, interview with Terence Higgins.

[21] Not until 1978 was the 'Operation of Lloyd's' course, which was designed for new staff in underwriters' boxes and agencies, divided into marine and non-marine courses. Lloyd's, *Annual Report for 1977–8*, 6, 8.

[22] Report of the Committee of Lloyd's 1976–7, in Lloyd's, *Minutes of the General Meeting*.

[23] Notes of Proceedings at a General Meeting, 30 June 1976, in Lloyd's, *Minutes of the General Meeting*.

held in the Room, that technical training must not be allowed to encroach upon or constrict traditional business practices.

Old attitudes to 'learning on the job' continued into the mid-1980s. In 1985, for example, Lloyd's Council considered a request to approve the appointment of a Mr B, with 'no first-hand underwriting experience', as the chief underwriter for a new non-marine syndicate, whose Names, as everywhere else in Lloyd's, had unlimited liability for any losses that their underwriter might produce. The request had been referred by Lloyd's Registration Committee to the Council, because guidance was sought on whether a principle should be established about the importance of first-hand underwriting experience. A lengthy debate in Council ensued, after which.

> there was general agreement that it would be unwise to state categorically that first-hand experience was essential for all proposed underwriters. It was felt that each case of this type should be judged on its merits.

It was resolved that in this case the application could not be approved 'until such time as Mr B. could demonstrate an acceptable level of underwriting experience'. The acceptable level for Mr B. was set at 12 months working as a deputy underwriter for the new syndicate, after which time 'the Committee felt that it would be a reasonable expectation that the application (to be the chief underwriter) would be approved'.[24]

Shortly after this debate, a 'Lloyd's Introductory Test', in a multiple choice format, was proposed for new users of the Room, on the grounds that there was a 'low level of knowledge among some younger people within the Market', and that 'it was generally acknowledged that the current level of knowledge among younger users of the Market was below standard'.[25] A few months later, the new Lloyd's Training Centre reported 'a lack of relevant training in certain areas' and that training needed to 'be more coordinated and efficient in the future'.[26] Yet there was opposition to the test from those who argued that it was the duty of employers, not Lloyd's Council, 'to determine who was or was not fitted

[24] Committee meetings 19 June, 25 June 1985, in Lloyd's, *Minutes of the Committee*, no.109; Council meeting 8 July 1985, in Lloyd's, *Minutes of Council*, no. 2. I have anonymised the individual concerned.

[25] Council meeting 5 August 1985, in Lloyd's, *Minutes of Council*, no. 2.

[26] Council meeting 14 October 1985, in Lloyd's, *Minutes of Council*, no. 2.

to conduct business in the Room'.[27] The test was introduced and made subject to a new byelaw; however, not everyone working in the Room was required to take it. Those whom the Council deemed to have 'sufficient experience' of insurance were exempt. Those who were not were given 15 months to pass it. The first Lloyd's Introductory Test was held in April 1986. With a failure rate of 26%, the results were regarded as 'generally disappointing'.[28] Finally, in 1987, a graduate training scheme was introduced for the Corporation, although its initial scope was modest: just ten graduates were to be selected through a series of 'exercises' from a field of 20 applicants, with a second class honours degree as a minimum entry requirement.[29] A common graduate recruiting scheme that also covered Lloyd's agents and brokers was not launched until 1994.[30]

Reading the discussions about training during the 1970s and 1980s, it is clear that traditional beliefs endured, namely that competency was best delivered through hands-on learning at an underwriter's box, without any kind of external control over the quality of that learning. Indeed, formal training, with courses and tests designed and operated by bodies outside the Room, was regarded as a threat to the 'flexibility' and independence of the underwriter. By the later 1980s, there was an increasing acceptance, driven not least by the scandals attributed not just to fraud but also to poor judgement, that underwriting had become more complicated and required more 'professional' skills than had been the case in the 1950s.[31] Nevertheless, up to the eve of the largest crisis in its 300-year history, many at Lloyd's continued to argue that competence should not be subject to external regulation or monitoring, but should only be assessed by the practitioners themselves and by their performance in the market.

Self-regulation, freedom of trade and non-interference in the independence of underwriters and brokers were the core principles of Lloyd's. They were repeated like mantras throughout the period at Committee and Council meetings, at general meetings of members, in exchanges with

[27] Council meeting 5 August 1985, in Lloyd's, *Minutes of Council*, no. 2.

[28] Council meetings 14 October, 9 December 1985, 12 May, 13 October 1986, in Lloyd's, *Minutes of Council*, no. 2.

[29] Council meeting 4 February 1987, in Lloyd's, *Minutes of Council*, no. 3.

[30] *Lloyd's Annual Report for 1994*.

[31] BL C409/027, interview with Terence Higgins.

government, Parliament and the press, and in public pronouncements. In its report for 1976, for example, the Committee declared that:

> By the long-held principle of unlimited financial responsibility, which is the bedrock of the Lloyd's market, by the ceaseless vigilance in the internal monitoring of the community's activities, and by the continued efforts of individual members in the self-regulation of Lloyd's affairs, the reputation of Lloyd's is sustained.[32]

Self-regulation, and the responsibility of the individual for his or her own economic decisions, had been a cornerstone of liberal ideology since the nineteenth century. It was manifested in commercial law, for instance, in the doctrine of *caveat emptor*. For these ideas to produce a successful, wealthy economy and a 'free' civil society, however, also required well informed citizens, and this in turn required publicity and transparency. One of the fathers of Victorian liberalism, the philosopher Jeremy Bentham, argued that secrecy bred injustice:

> In the darkness of secrecy, sinister interest, and evil in every shape have full swing. Only in proportion as publicity has place can any of the checks applicable to judicial injustice operate. Where there is no publicity there is no justice. Publicity is the very soul of justice...It keeps the judge himself while trying under trial.[33]

The Times, in an article of 1850, agreed: 'Incompetence loves secrecy – idleness loves secrecy – corruption loves secrecy'.[34] For Lloyd's, however, secrecy had always been key to their claims that self-regulation was their optimal form of governance. Underwriting in the Room, it was repeatedly claimed, should not be interfered with because outsiders, including state legislators, could not be expected to understand its complexities. Francis Holford, who worked in the Lloyd's Information Department in the 1950s, described its mission as being 'to give away as little information about Lloyd's as possible. They were not a publicity-seeking

[32] Report of the Committee of Lloyd's 1976, 1, in Lloyd's, *Minutes of the General Meeting*.

[33] Bentham, *Rationale of Judicial Evidence*, i, c. 10. Cf. also Biagini, 'Liberalism'.

[34] *The Times* 21 September 1850.

organisation'.[35] Thus, there was a contradiction at the core of Lloyd's political economy, between, on the one hand, the liberal espousal of self-governance and the principle of individual responsibility enshrined in the freedom of underwriters and the unlimited liability of Names, and, on the other hand, the secrecy and lack of information about market and governance practices that were also proclaimed as virtues by the leaders of Lloyd's.

As Lloyd's membership grew to many thousands, pressure came from two directions to abandon this position. First, many of the new Names who joined Lloyd's expected a greater flow of information about the market that they were investing in. Second, there was a growing political interest in consumer protection generally, and this eventually stretched to include the welfare of investors at Lloyd's. In 1986, for instance, Lloyd's Council discussed a proposal to introduce a code of practice for managing agents rather than compelling them to provide Names with greater information about the underwriting of their syndicates. Sir Kenneth Berrill, who joined the Council having been chief secretary to the Treasury, contrasted the proposal unfavourably with the improvements in the amount and quality of information available in the shares and securities markets, and expressed concern that Lloyd's intended 'not to make significantly more information available to enable Names to make comparisons of agents with a view to transferring from one to another'.[36]

There was considerable resistance, however, to any movement towards greater transparency that required direct intervention or compulsion. In 1985, for instance, a working party recommended that 'errors and omissions' (E&O) insurance be made a requirement to protect Names against dishonesty by their underwriting agents, and that a central 'fraud fund' be established by Lloyd's. This was opposed by several members of Council, who argued that the mutuality that such a fund would involve was 'inappropriate' for the Lloyd's market, and that it was not correct 'that (other) Agents and Names should pay large sums of money for those Names who had misjudged the honesty of their Agents'. Moreover, 'the overwhelming view was that underwriters should not be obliged to advise Names of the level of E&O cover that they have purchased', because

[35] BL C409/067, interview with Francis Holford.

[36] Council meeting 10 November 1986, in Lloyd's, *Minutes of Council*, no. 2.

such a revelation might jeopardise recruitment to syndicates.[37] In short, the majority view remained that Lloyd's was a free market that investors entered at their peril, with limited information about the unlimited risks that they were undertaking, and without any guarantees of being rescued should their syndicates fail.

A further example of this attitude can be found in the deliberations, also in 1985,

over a proposal to introduce 'consumer guarantees' into Lloyd's general policies, in the wake of the so-called 'Multi-Guarantee' fraud that had aroused considerable public and political interest.[38] Voices were raised against the proposal as an example of 'undesirable interference with underwriting judgment'. The questions posed by the fraud 'were all matters which the market should be left to decide without bureaucratic interference'. The chair of Council, Peter Miller, however, pointed out that 'the likelihood of public and political action in this field made it desirable for Lloyd's to be ready with well-argued views about those aspects which affected the consumer interest' 'Consumerism', he suggested, 'was an irresistible political tide'. As often happened with proposals to introduce any monitoring of practices in the Room, a decision was put off by referring the issue to a working party.[39]

Similar arguments for non-interference based on a defence of underwriters' liberty were evident in the long running debate about whether Lloyd's governing body should regulate the size of syndicates. By 1977, Lloyd's Committee were becoming increasingly nervous about the rising tide of new applications for membership. So many applications were being received that the traditional method of approving new Names, the

[37] Committee meeting 23 October 1985, in Lloyd's, *Minutes of the Committee,* no.109.

[38] Multi-Guarantee was a company owned by a crook called Ronald Meddes, who used his position as a member of Lloyd's to help sell a fraudulent extended warranty scheme, backed by non-existent insurance cover from Lloyd's, to a major UK electrical goods retailer. See *Multi-Guarantee Ltd versus The Companies Act 1948*, heard at the Court of Appeal 17 April 1986, which outlines the fraud. Long after he was expelled from Lloyd's, Meddes made the news again in 2014, when he and his wife Regina Lansley, a self-styled socialite—the press inevitably named them 'Ron and Reg'—were sentenced to jail for a £5.9m black market scam selling illegal veterinary medicines out of their farmhouse in France. squaremilenews.blogspot.com, 24 February 2014; *La Semaine Vétérinaire* no. 1463, 23 September 2011; Interpol, *Against Organised Crime: Interpol Trafficking and Counterfeiting Casebook 2014*, p. 60. www.interpol.int, accessed 27 July 2021.

[39] Council meeting 11 February 1985, in Lloyd's, *Minutes of Council,* no. 2.

individual interview by the so-called 'Rota Committee', was abandoned and group interviews of several applicants at a time were introduced, as a 'matter of expedience'. Lloyd's Committee recognised the conflict of interest that was emerging between, on the one hand, members' agents whose earnings were geared to the numbers they recruited—each new member bringing additional insurance capacity to their syndicates—and, on the other hand, underwriters trying to keep their underwriting levels within safe limits. Despite this recognition, the independence of the Room remained paramount, and the only solution offered was not regulation, but advice to agents to 'act responsibly':

> ...it is the view of the Committee of Lloyd's that it should not interfere in the business of underwriting agents, the decision as to how much additional capacity can be accepted being a business decision. It is therefore up to underwriting agents to act responsibly in this matter: naturally this entails accepting the advice of the actual underwriters in the various markets, and not bringing pressure on them to increase their premium income against their better judgment.[40]

In 1978, the principle of non-interference was reiterated in the evidence given by Lloyd's Committee to the Wilson Inquiry on City financial institutions. The Committee confirmed that it saw itself largely as having a public relations role, with its priority being to protect the reputation of Lloyd's and to market its services around the world, but not to interfere in the underwriting by syndicates, nor in their decisions about whether to increase premium capacity by taking on new members, what to insure and under what policy conditions, and what premium rates to charge.

> The power and authority vested in the Chairman and Committee of Lloyd's does not...extend to the daily running of the underwriting business. It is dissimilar in most respects to the board of directors of a company. This is clear to those who live and work at Lloyd's. It is our continuing concern to make this clear to the rest of the world.[41]

[40] Notes of Proceedings at a General Meeting, 22 June 1977, in Lloyd's, *Minutes of the General Meeting*.

[41] Lloyd's, *Annual Report for 1977–8*, 5.

Lloyd's chairman, Ian Findlay, under pressure in the wake of the Sasse Turnbull scandal (described in the following chapter), several times repeated the message that the Committee could not set underwriting limits for syndicates. The Committee's role, he stated, was to ensure that the premium limits for individual Names matched the amount of assets that they put up to back their underwriting, and that in this way it was safeguarding the security behind Lloyd's policies.[42] This was a dubious assertion because the ability of any syndicate to pay claims was dependent on: first, the underwriter not issuing policies beyond the total capacity of his syndicate, and, as noted, Lloyd's Committee refused to exercise any control over the relation between insurance written and each syndicate's underwriting capacity; second, the underwriter not writing insurance on risks that he had misunderstood or mis-estimated; third, reinsurers paying up on their liabilities for any risks reinsured by the underwriter; fourth, the failure of one syndicate to pay large losses, which, as events in the late 1980s demonstrated, could result in a loss of confidence in the entire Lloyd's market.

Resistance to any degree of interference by Lloyd's governing body in the operations of syndicates, underwriters and brokers proved enormously difficult to break down. In 1986, Lloyd's Solvency and Security Committee presented a series of clear rules governing member's deposits and annual means test, with the aim of preventing syndicates writing above their capacity. Lloyd's Council did on this occasion accept 'the inevitability of a maximum overall limit...even though it might be difficult to justify in philosophical terms (in that this should be determined by market forces)'. It was conceded that 'if no overall limit were in force, underwriting may be heavily concentrated in individual Names'.[43]

In sum, on the eve of the greatest sequence of underwriting losses in Lloyd's history, many traditional attitudes persisted. The political economy of Lloyd's consisted of a few simple beliefs rooted in Victorian liberalism: the belief in the sacrosanct freedom of the market in the Room; the belief that efficiency, flexibility and innovation were best maintained by leaving underwriters and brokers alone, to conduct insurance as they saw fit, without outside interference, either by the officers

[42] Notes of Proceedings at a General Meeting, 21 June 1978, 27 June, 7 November 1979, in Lloyd's, *Minutes of the General Meeting*.

[43] Council meeting 9 June 1986, in Lloyd's, *Minutes of Council*, no. 2.

of Lloyd's, who saw their role as largely promotional and administrative rather than managerial, or by external bodies such as Parliament; the belief that competence was gained by hands-on experience at the underwriter's box, rather than by formal education delivered outside the Room; and the belief that the precious right of self-regulation, and Lloyd's global reputation, was best preserved by ensuring that, as far as possible, Lloyd's remained a secretive and mysterious place of ancient practices, a 'stuffy' place somewhat separate from the rest of the City, difficult to penetrate by the light of external criticism and investigation.[44]

[44] BL C409/033, interview with Gwilym H. Lewis; C409/026, interview with Leonard Toomey; C409/067, interview with Francis Holford; Davison, 'Affadivit'.

CHAPTER 4

Expansion, Scandals and Frauds—Lloyd's in the 1970s

Abstract By the late 1960s, the growth in large risks such as supertankers and losses from natural disasters led to calls to increase the underwriting capacity of the Lloyd's market. As the traditional entry restrictions were removed, ever larger numbers joined Lloyd's, attracted by years of sustained profits and by the tax advantages associated with membership. This rapid expansion brought a number of new challenges, including pressure for greater representation of non-working members on the Committee of Lloyd's. While new members flooded into Lloyd's, the market began to suffer an unprecedented series of frauds, scandals and accusations of negligent underwriting. These problems pushed the Committee, reluctantly, into ever more supervisory and disciplinary acts of intervention to sustain the reputation of the market and protect the principle of self-governance from those who were calling for greater external scrutiny of Lloyd's practices.

Keyword Lloyd's of London · Natural disasters · Governance · Fraud · Financial crime

R. Pearson, *Delusions of Competence*,
Palgrave Studies in Economic History,
https://doi.org/10.1007/978-3-030-94088-1_4

By the end of the 1960s, the growth in large risks such as super-tankers and jet aircraft, and the losses associated with Hurricane Betsy, which damaged shipyards and oil refineries along the US Gulf coast in 1965, raised Lloyd's awareness of the need to increase the underwriting capacity of the market. Hurricane Betsy, in particular, led to three consecutive years of losses at Lloyd's 1965–1967, and the exit of members, a decline that was not reversed until 1971.[1] Other external factors also drove Lloyd's to search for new capacity. These included new Lloyd's-type insurance exchanges being set up in New York, Chicago and Florida to capture some of Lloyd's market share, and the nationalist legislation being passed by post-colonial states that limited the amount of insurance that Lloyd's could write directly in their countries.[2] Lloyd's became engaged in an almost continual series of negotiations with foreign governments to protect its access to direct insurance markets in places such as Kenya, Italy, Spain and Greece, while also lobbying in the USA, Canada and the European Economic Community to become an accredited reinsurer in those markets.[3]

In 1969, an inquiry was commissioned from the Earl of Cromer to examine the ways in which Lloyd's might increase its membership. Cromer recommended lowering the means-tested qualification for Names and introducing a new simplified deposit scheme.[4] Membership was opened to all nationalities and to women. The result was a surge in applications, further stimulated by successive years of record profits 1971–3—though much of the profits derived from higher investment yields and reduced expenses rather than from underwriting—and by the tax advantages associated with membership.[5] Syndicate earnings were placed directly into Lloyd's Special Reserve Fund, in return for which Names received a bond. Accrued interest from the bond was taxed as capital

[1] Davison, *Lloyd's*, p. 43; BL C409/027, interview with Terence Higgins.

[2] On insurance exchanges in New York and elsewhere, see *The Times* 31 March 1980, 15 July 1981. These were actually exchanges with syndicates funded by corporate members with limited liability, so they differed in that regard from Lloyd's of London.

[3] Report of the Committee of Lloyd's 1976–7, in Lloyd's, *Minutes of the General Meeting*; Lloyd's, *Annual Report for 1979*, 7.

[4] *The Times* 9 April 1970, 11 August, 4 November 1975. Cromer's report also criticised the way that Lloyd's was organised and the quality of information made available to Names, but this was ignored (the report was never published).

[5] *The Times* 27 August 1976.

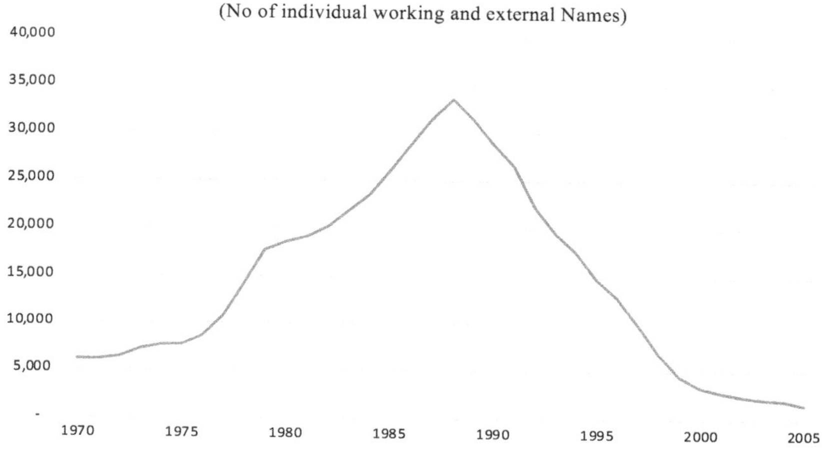

Fig. 4.1 Membership of Lloyd's 1970–2005

gains, the rate of which was considerably lower than the highest levels of personal income tax. This system of so-called 'bond washing' helped wealthy Names avoid paying the higher band of UK income tax, which rose continuously through the 1970s until it exceeded, in some cases, 60%.[6] A further attraction of becoming a Name was that much syndicate income was denominated in US $, which appreciated against £ sterling throughout the period.

In 1970, at the time of the Cromer report, there were 6,000 Names at Lloyd's. Within ten years, the number had trebled (see Fig. 4.1). This rapid expansion allowed more insurance to be written, but also brought a number of new challenges. It put pressure on physical space, which directly led to the commissioning of a new building at 1 Lime Street,

[6] A fierce, but ultimately vain, action to defend bond-washing was fought in 1985 when the UK Inland Revenue declared their intention to apply income tax rates rather than the capital gains tax rate to the interest from Lloyd's bonds. At the time, it was estimated that this switch in tax rates would cost Names an additional £70m, or a 30% increase in their tax burden. Committee meeting 6 March 1985, in Lloyd's, *Minutes of the Committee,* no.109. On bond washing and Lloyd's campaign against the tax changes in the 1985 budget, see Council meetings 15 April, 13 May, 17 June 1985, in Lloyd's, *Minutes of Council,* no. 2.

opened in 1986 at a far greater cost than had first been anticipated.[7] The growth in business produced a rising level of criticism from policyholders of the way that Lloyd's handled the routines of insurance, especially the delays in paying claims.[8] The existing telephone exchange was found incapable of coping with the new volume of traffic and had to be replaced. A new computerised data entry system was introduced in the Policy Signing Office, with VDUs linked to DEC 1170 mini-computers. These allowed the operator to record details of each transaction between underwriters and brokers, and enabled errors to be corrected quickly and the policy signing process to be speeded up.[9] The influx of new Names, most of whom were largely unfamiliar with Lloyd's traditional ways, led to increasing demands for greater representation of non-working Names on the Lloyd's Committee—'no taxation without representation', as one member put it—and greater powers of governance, such as the power to propose byelaws, rather than just the power to veto byelaws proposed by the Council. This pressure emerged most clearly in the debates in 1980 about the new Lloyd's parliamentary bill (discussed in the following chapter), when several members attending an Extraordinary General Meeting in the Royal Albert Hall called for the establishment of an Association of External Names that could lobby on behalf of its members.[10] This increased political power of non-working Names, a new phenomenon in the history of Lloyd's, was to become significant in the crisis later in the 1980s.

While new members flooded into Lloyd's, the market began to suffer an unprecedented series of tanker, oil rig and aviation disasters, scandals

[7] In 1978, the cost had initially been estimated at £40 m. By 1982, the cost had soared to £157 m. Lloyd's, *Annual Report for 1979*, 9; Council meeting 14 October 1985, in Lloyd's, *Minutes of Council*, no. 2. Not everyone at Lloyd's was happy with what they got for their money—Richard Rogers' 14-storeyed 'inside-out' building with external glass lifts.

[8] Notes of Proceedings at a General Meeting, 18 June 1980, in Lloyd's, *Minutes of the General Meeting*.

[9] Lloyd's, *Annual Report for 1977–8*, 6, 8.

[10] Notes of Proceedings at an Extraordinary General Meeting, 4 November 1980, in Lloyd's, *Minutes of the General Meeting*. The Association, chaired by Lady Janet Middleton, was founded shortly after the Albert Hall meeting. Middleton was a Name in the Sasse syndicate, the scandal about which is discussed below.

and accusations of negligent underwriting and poor monitoring of syndicates.[11] Shipping losses in the Iran-Iraq War between 1979 and 1982, and huge losses on computer leasing insurance in the US—estimated in 1979 to be $220 m—compounded the effect of the disasters and scandals.[12]

One of the first major scandals of the period related to a cargo ship, the *Savonita*, which in 1978 sailed with a consignment of over 2,000 Fiat cars from Italy to the USA.[13] After eight hours at sea, a fire was discovered on the cargo deck and extinguished, but some cars were said to be damaged by fire, smoke and water. The ship returned to port and unloaded 301 allegedly damaged cars. The cars had been insured by SIAT, a Fiat-controlled marine insurance company, which in turn had reinsured the policies with Lloyd's and the Institute of London Underwriters' Companies (ILU). The London reinsurers were consequently presented with a claim for £500,000. The reinsurers were immediately suspicious and so were the small firm of London brokers, Pearson Webb Springbett (PWS), who were acting on behalf of SIAT. A team of investigators, together with an ex-CID officer, went to Italy and uncovered evidence that it was a fraud. The 301 cars that were written off had been sold at 15% of their value to a Fiat dealer in Naples, and then resold by him for 80% of their brand new value to various customers, apparently with the connivance of several Fiat executives. The London underwriters, therefore, resisted the claim and refused to offer more than 10% in settlement to SIAT. Representatives of PWS went to see Lloyd's chairman, Havelock Hudson, about the claim, who rather unhelpfully but characteristically told them to 'bat straight'. At this point, SIAT dismissed PWS and appointed the major broking firm of Willis Faber to handle the claim, and they eventually managed to collect 96% of the reinsurance claim from Lloyd's and the ILU. With excess capacity in the London market at the time, both company and syndicate underwriters were fearful of losing large accounts

[11] The *Amoco Cadiz*, for example, broke up in a storm in 1978, leaking 230,000 tons of oil onto the beaches of Brittany. This cost Lloyd's over $31 m, including payments into a French government fund to compensate Bretons for sea pollution. *The Times* 18 March, 29 April, 2 October, 13 November 1978, 5 November 1980, 21 April 1984.

[12] Notes of Proceedings at a General Meeting, 7 November 1979, in Lloyd's, *Minutes of the General Meeting*.

[13] The following is drawn from the account of the fraud given by Jonathan Aitken in the House of Commons adjournment debate, *House of Commons Debates*, 23 March 1978, vol. 946, cc. 1755–72.

and were therefore vulnerable to pressure for the generous settlement of dubious claims. The Conservative MP for Thanet East, Jonathan Aitken, himself a Name, accused Lloyd's of weak management and failing to protect its small investors. Although a defender of the independence of Lloyd's, he regarded the *Savonita* fraud as evidence that improvements in its system of self-policing were needed. The response from the Labour government and from other Conservative MPs was that the fraud was a police matter and that Lloyd's history of self-regulation was 'exemplary'. Lloyd's Committee nevertheless established an internal inquiry into the handling of the *Savonita* claim, and conclusions drawn from this, regarding the need for the Committee to have greater powers to monitor behaviour in the market, were fed into the new Lloyd's parliamentary bill of 1980 (discussed in the following chapter).[14]

The most significant scandal emerged from the syndicate Sasse, Turnbull and Co., which was suspended in 1977 when its members formed an action group and refused to pay calls. Two years earlier, Tim Sasse, the chief underwriter, had authorised the Den-Har Underwriters' Agency, run by a Florida-based expatriate called Dennis Harrison, to write insurance on his syndicate's behalf under a procedure known as a 'binding authority', even though Den-Har was not an approved Lloyd's coverholder, a fact noticed neither by Sasse nor by Lloyd's.[15] The story later emerged that the Den-Har deal was concluded not at Lloyd's but at a wine bar around the corner in Billiter Street, where Sasse allegedly held court every afternoon over large glasses of vintage port.[16] Harrison, who had supposed mafia links, placed large volumes of property insurance on derelict housing in South Bronx slums and similar areas elsewhere in the US and Canada. A number of the insured properties soon burned down at a cost of £25m, and the 110 Names on Sasse's syndicate 762 were told

[14] Lloyd's, *Annual Report for 1979*.

[15] 'Cover-holders' were local agents (they could be companies or individuals) granted authority from Lloyd's to write insurance on behalf of Lloyd's syndicates.

[16] Andrew Newman, 'Round the corner', *Insurance People* (April 2015): 30. Frederick Hugh (Tim) Sasse (1924–1987) was also one of the underwriters on syndicates that had written loss-making 'computer leasing' policies in the late 1970s. One of his passions was racehorses. In 1973, he bought *Coup de Feu* for 26,000 guineas as a gift to his son Duncan, who was starting a new career as a trainer. In 1974, at 33–1, *Coup de feu* became the longest priced winner in the history of the Eclipse Stakes at Sandown. https://crossgategallery.com/product/coup-de-feu, accessed 15 July 2021.

that they faced substantial losses from mostly fraudulent claims. Sasse's Brazilian reinsurer refused to pay its share of the losses.

In 1980, the Sasse Names sued Lloyd's, alleging a failure of supervision. Under the pressure of the legal requirement to provide to the UK Department of Trade a certificated audit of the Sasse Turnbull accounts, and under the threat of further legal action by the Names to prevent Lloyd's using their deposits and assets to pay the claims on the Den-Har policies, Lloyd's decided to offer a loan of £3.2m to the Sasse Names, which they could place with their syndicate to get its accounts past the audit.[17] In return for both sides suspending legal action against each other, the Sasse Names were asked to submit to judicial arbitration of their disputed liabilities. An out-of-court agreement was eventually reached in 1983 with all but a few of the litigants, by which Lloyd's shouldered 58% of the combined losses of £21.5m on syndicate 762's accounts for 1976 and 1977.[18] The outstanding liabilities were placed in a new vehicle, Additional Underwriters Agency 2 (AUA2), one of several that Lloyd's had to create over the following decade to manage the run-off business of failed syndicates. AUA2 was still managing the run-off of Sasse Turnbull risks at the end of the 1980s, which indicates how long lasting the effects of such failures could be.[19]

Disciplinary proceedings were begun against Sasse and one of his partners, J. H. Newman, which dragged on into 1985. This caused Tim Sasse great distress—he was to die only a few years later. When Lloyd's chairman, Peter Green, approached Sasse to ask for his cooperation in resolving the litigation by the Names, he found him 'in an emotional state and it was very difficult to obtain a satisfactory reaction'.[20] At one point, the Investigations Committee considered discontinuing the proceedings 'on humanitarian grounds', but decided against doing so.[21] Sasse pleaded

[17] The loan was listed in the Consolidated Balance Sheet for 1979 as a 'bank overdraft'. Lloyd's, *Annual Report for 1980*, 12.

[18] Notes of Proceedings at a General Meeting, 19 November 1980, in Lloyd's, *Minutes of the General Meeting*; *The Times* 25 July 1980; Council meeting 18 April 1983, in Lloyd's, *Minutes of Council, no.1.* Lloyd's recovered $7m of this from Sasse's Brazilian reinsurer in 1981. *The Times* 18 June 1981. See also the account in Luessenhop, *Risky Business*, 135–9.

[19] Council meeting 5 April 1989, in Lloyd's, *Minutes of Council,* no. 5.

[20] Council meeting 18 April 1983, in Lloyd's, *Minutes of Council,* no. 1.

[21] Council meeting 9 April 1984, in Lloyd's, *Minutes of Council,* no. 1.

guilty to all the charges of 'discreditable conduct' brought against him and was suspended from transacting any business at Lloyd's, except as an individual member on his own account. Newman was excluded for life from transacting business at Lloyd's, but was permitted to requalify as an external (non-working) member of the Society. Sasse was distraught at the damage that the suspension did to his reputation. He pointed out that he had not misappropriated any funds and alleged that the proceedings against him were unfair. Lloyd's chairman Peter Miller noted that Sasse had pleaded guilty to all charges, which countered his allegations of unfairness, since he could have chosen to defend himself.[22]

The risk of reputational damage from the threatened litigation by Sasse Names was the key to Lloyd's landmark decisions in the affair. It was the first time for many years that Lloyd's had been forced to intervene in what Terence Higgins called 'a case of thoroughly bad underwriting', where Lloyd's rules (about binding authorities) had been broken.[23] The bailout of the Names on syndicate 762 marked a breach in the much vaunted principles of the unlimited liability of Names and non-interference in the operations of the Room. After Sasse Turnbull, it became much harder for the Corporation of Lloyd's to reject responsibility for the oversight of underwriting by individual syndicates on the grounds that the freedom of the market was sacrosanct.

[22] Council meeting 13 May 1985; Special Council meeting 9 September 1985, in Lloyd's, *Minutes of Council*, no. 2.

[23] BL C409/027, interview with Terence Higgins.

CHAPTER 5

The First Reforms and Public Scrutiny

Abstract The scandals of the late 1970s drew attention to several issues that dogged Lloyd's through the following decade: the efficacy of its governance system, the problematic relationship between members, their underwriters and the managing agents of their syndicates, and the conflict of interest implicit in broking firms placing business with syndicates that they owned. The Fisher report into Lloyd's governance structure made important recommendations, some of which became incorporated into the new Lloyd's Act of 1982. These recommendations included divestment, forcing Lloyd's brokers to sell off their underwriting interests, and the establishment of a new governing body for Lloyd's, the Council, with wider representation of groups that were not market insiders. The Act was extensively debated by the British parliament, but most legislators continued to be convinced that, with the implementation of the reforms, Lloyd's remained competent to govern itself.

Keywords Lloyd's Act of 1982 · Conflicts of Interest · Fisher Report · Divestment · Self-regulation

R. Pearson, *Delusions of Competence*,
Palgrave Studies in Economic History,
https://doi.org/10.1007/978-3-030-94088-1_5

Such scandals drew attention to several issues that dogged Lloyd's through the 1980s: the efficacy of its governance system, the problematic relationship between Names, their underwriters and the managing agents of their syndicates, and the conflict of interest implicit in broking firms placing business with syndicates that they owned. The continued entry of large numbers of new Names, many of them ignorant of the insurance business and not very rich, made these issues more pressing. The Sasse Turnbull affair, in particular, suggested to some that the monitoring and disciplinary powers accorded by the Lloyd's Act of 1871 to the governing body of Lloyd's, the Committee, were insufficient if Lloyd's reputation was to be protected from damaging scandals in the Room, and its funds were to be protected from costly law suits by disgruntled Names. As Peter Miller later recalled: 'There was an increasing sense that people weren't going to do what the Committee said, particularly in the resolution of disputes'.[1]

In 1979, a working party was appointed to look into these matters, chaired by former High Court Judge Sir Henry Fisher. Fisher reported in 1980 with 79 recommendations for improvements in Lloyd's governance structure. The major recommendations were (i) the expansion of the Committee into a new governing body, a Council, to include non-executive directors, and with greater disciplinary and regulatory powers to be made explicit in a new Lloyd's Act; (ii) divestment, forcing Lloyd's brokers to sell off their underwriting interests within five years; (iii) divorce of members' agents from managing agents, i.e. preventing agents who recruited names for syndicates from managing those syndicates.[2]

The first of Fisher's main recommendations was inserted into a parliamentary bill, approved by an overwhelming vote of members at an Extraordinary General Meeting of Lloyd's members held in Royal Albert Hall in November 1980. The bill included a controversial clause that stated:

> Neither the Society nor any of its officers or employees shall be under any liability for negligence or other tort, breach of statutory duty, or on any other ground whatsoever to any member of the Society, Lloyd's Broker, Underwriting Agent, or partner of a Lloyd's Broker or Underwriting

[1] BL C409/015, interview with Sir Peter Miller.

[2] Lloyd's, *Self-Regulation at Lloyd's*. On managing agents and members' agents, see Chapter 2, p. 12.

Agent, or any person who works for a Lloyd's Broker or Underwriting Agent.

In defending the clause, Lloyd's chairman Peter Green cited the Fisher report, namely that '...it would be contrary to the public interest if the Corporation of Lloyd's was to be inhibited in the task of self-regulation by fear of legal proceedings against it'. The aim of the bill and its new liability clause, Green explained, was to make self-regulation more effective, by not constraining the powers of the new Council to investigate and to discipline market behaviour, and thereby to reduce the scope for calls for external regulation.[3]

The Lloyd's private bill was introduced by Sir Graham Page, Conservative MP for Crosby, in the House of Commons early in 1981.[4] It took up considerable parliamentary time. At its second reading in the Commons in March, the Conservative benches were packed.[5] Introducing the bill, Page cited Fisher: 'Things go wrong because Lloyd's has an antiquated constitution and restricted powers of regulation over its community'. The Lloyd's Act of 1871 had been passed at a time when Lloyd's had fewer than 1,000 members. It was not suited to an institution of over 19,000 names, most of whom had no experience of the market. Under the existing Act, every disciplinary proceeding against a member had to be heard by two arbitrators, whose rulings had to be confirmed by two successive general meetings. The Sasse case could have been dealt with more quickly, and to the satisfaction of all Names, had the powers in the new bill existed. Moreover, the 1871 Act gave Lloyd's no powers over brokers; in fact, it did not mention brokers at all.

The front benches of the Conservative government and the Labour opposition broadly agreed on the need to preserve the principle of

[3] Notes of Proceedings at an Extraordinary General Meeting, 4 November 1980, in Lloyd's, Minutes of the General Meeting.

[4] In British parliamentary procedure, a 'private bill' is one introduced by individuals or bodies outside Parliament with a view to obtaining powers beyond those provided by the normal law of the land. It should not be confused with a 'private member's bill' which is a public bill introduced by a private Member of Parliament not by the government, and intended to change UK statute law. Page died early in 1982 and the sponsorship of Lloyd's bill was taken over by Sir Anthony Grant, Conservative MP for Harrow Central.

[5] The following account is based on *House of Commons Debates* 24 March 1981, vol. 1, cc. 859–94.

self-regulation. There was little doubt among the majority of parliamentarians at the time that Lloyd's had the competence to govern its own affairs, once it was given fuller powers over its members and the most overt conflicts of interest were removed. Reginald Eyre, Under-Secretary of State for Trade, was typical of this view when he proclaimed that 'Lloyd's owes its character as an institution to the fact that it is self-regulating…Government regulation could not be substituted for self-regulation without destroying the character of the institution'.[6] Only some on the Labour left had reservations about granting powers to an outside body without any means of supervising it in the public interest.[7] The Conservative back benches, where over 50 Names sat, were united behind self-regulation, but disunited on what that should mean in practice. Some wanted greater accountability. Some joined a campaign, organised by Lady Middleton's Association of External Names, against the clause in the bill that granted the new Lloyd's Council what some saw as 'blanket immunity' against legal action. Others could not see what the fuss was about. If Names wanted protection, 'they shouldn't have joined Lloyds in the first place'.[8] In the end, an amendment was agreed that safeguarded the Council against litigation by Names for negligent or fraudulent underwriting by their syndicates, but removed its immunity from claims deriving from its own negligence.[9]

When the bill moved to the committee stage, the key concerns of parliamentarians centred on the need to protect Lloyd's members and mitigate the power of the large brokers. The House of Commons committee, chaired by the Labour MP Michael Meacher, demanded that two important recommendations of Fisher, divestment and divorce, be inserted into the bill. This provoked a furious debate within Lloyd's. Lloyd's Committee did not welcome either demand, but had reluctantly to accept that there was a case for divestment and that there was a

[6] *House of Commons Debates* 24 March 1981, vol. 1, 867–8 (Eyre).

[7] *House of Commons Debates* 24 March 1981, vol. 1, cc. 881–3 (Cryer).

[8] *The Times* 23 February 1981. On the Association of External Names, see the letter to *The Times* 16 March 1981. On opposition to the immunity clause, see *House of Commons Debates* 24 March 1981, vol. 1, c. 880–3, 888–90; ibid., 22 February 1982, vol. 18, cc. 686–720.

[9] Eliz. II (1982) XIV, (the Lloyd's Act) clause 14. *The Times* 15 July 1981; *House of Commons Debates* 3 February 1982, vol. 17, c. 370 (Grant), c. 392 (Eyre); ibid., 22 February 1982, vol. 18, c. 697 (Aitken), cc. 688–9 (Bonsor), cc. 712–14 (Grant).

conflict of interest where brokers, seeking insurance cover on behalf of their clients, also owned the managing agencies of the syndicates that underwrote the cover. The Committee remained opposed, however, to the demand for the divorce of members' agents from managing agents, claiming that there was no conflict of interest about which legislators needed to be concerned. At a general meeting of members in June 1981, called to vote on the demands, Green advised that in order to save the bill from being rejected by Parliament, Lloyd's might have to swallow the divestment of brokers, but that a large vote against the divorce of managing agents from members' agents would maximise the chance of avoiding this demand. Lloyd's argument was that, while divestment involved the public in the form of policyholders, divorce only affected the members of Lloyd's, and therefore, this should remain within the compass of self-regulation and not be the subject of interference by the state or an external body. In short, Lloyd's tactics were to circle the wagons around the principle of self-regulation, while giving up ground in areas where Lloyd's operations spilled over into (what others defined as) areas of public interest. The members subsequently voted heavily in favour of divestment but rejected divorce.[10] Meacher's committee accepted the vote and abandoned the demand for a divorce clause, in return for a promise that, once the bill has passed through Parliament, the new Lloyd's Council would pass a byelaw requiring better disclosure of information to members.[11]

Several powerful broking firms, including Alexander Howden, C.E. Heath and Minet Holdings, resolved to fight the divestment clause by petitioning Parliament. They claimed that the views of brokers had not been heard properly, and that divestment would hamper Lloyd's competitiveness abroad.[12] More implausibly, those who represented the brokers' case in the Commons argued, in the face of majority opinion and the evidence presented in both the Fisher and Cromer reports, that there was no conflict of interest between underwriters and brokers and that Lloyd's was not dominated by the large broking firms.[13] Michael Meacher

[10] Notes of Proceedings at a General Meeting, 9 June 1981, in Lloyd's, Minutes of the General Meeting, p. 9; *The Times* 15 July, 17 July 1981.

[11] *The Times* 21 July 1981.

[12] *The Times* 15 July, 8 December 1981.

[13] Cf. the contribution of Roger Moate, MP for Faversham, in *House of Commons Debates* 22 February 1982 vol. 18, cc. 666–7. Moate, who was a director of a subsidiary

responded by pointing to that fact that 59% of total premiums at Lloyds were already now controlled by the eight largest broking firms, and that of the total reinsurance orders handled by the Posgate underwriting syndicate within Alexander Howden, no less than 58% went through the Alexander Howden brokers: '…I do not believe that such a situation is compatible with the absolute guarantee of arm's length transactions that is needed. That revelation in itself goes a long way to demonstrate why nothing short of full divestment will secure that guarantee'.[14]

Not all brokers opposed divestment. Ian Posgate, Howden's chief underwriter at Lloyd's—nicknamed 'Goldfinger' for the huge profits made by his syndicates—was 'openly and vehemently' in favour of divestment.[15] In his evidence to Meacher's committee, Posgate had drawn attention to:

> …several abuses, which in his experience had occurred because of the broker ownership and control of underwriting syndicates. Those included large discounts for brokerages of up to 40 per cent to 60 per cent, brokers placing business with their controlled syndicates on terms other than the best market terms, erratic ratings, the taking of a profit commission by the broker on the underwriting result, the misallocation of expenses between the Names in the syndicate and the broking company and the payment of large commissions for the introduction of Names.

Posgate also argued that if compulsory divestment was not included in the bill, Lloyd's Council would not impose it themselves because of vested interests. Peter Miller, with the benefit of hindsight, later commented that Posgate had taken this stance, not on any ethical grounds, but because he was one of Lloyd's most powerful underwriters. If divestment was enforced by law, Posgate would have his employers, Howden, 'over a barrel', be able to carry out a management buy-out of his syndicates for

of Alexander Howden but not himself a member of Lloyd's, tabled an amendment, in vain, to make divestment in the first instance a matter for Lloyd's rather than a statutory mandate.

[14] *House of Commons Debates* 22 February 1982, vol. 18, c. 677 (Meacher).

[15] Posgate's marine insurance syndicate, managed by the Alexander Howden brokerage firm, had almost doubled its premium income in 1979 from £39.9m to £61.3m, and retained its top spot as the largest earner at Lloyd's. It was estimated that Posgate, who had been working at Lloyd's for 18 years, had written £100m of premium income in that time. *The Times* 26 August 1982.

very little and make himself very rich as a result.[16] Events were soon to cast Posgate in an even more unfavourable light (see the following chapter).

The Lloyd's bill passed its third Commons reading with the divestment clause intact, and passed to the Lords, where an even larger number of members of Lloyd's (194) sat than in the House of Commons.[17] The Labour opposition supported the bill. Labour Lord Mishcon hailed Lloyd's as a 'great national institution...which has carried British integrity throughout the world...'.[18] Some peers who had lost money in the Sasse affair again called for a removal of the immunity clause, but the Lords select committee reported in favour of the bill.[19] It passed its third reading in the Lords in July 1982 and shortly after was signed into law.

The Lloyd's Act that came into effect from January 1983 thus contained divestment and immunity provisions, but no divorce clause.[20] It authorised a Council of 27, 16 of whom were to be elected by the working names—about 20% of the total—with eight members being elected by postal ballot of the other four-fifths of 'external' names not working in the market.[21] The remaining three members, intended to be independent, were to be nominated by the Bank of England. The new Council was more representative of Lloyd's Society than the old Committee, which had been elected only by working members. Nevertheless, it was still stacked in favour of Lloyd's insiders, and, importantly, it had the power to delegate decisions to a committee of its working members. The Council was to have powers to make byelaws by special resolution, so that the general meeting of members ceased to be the primary rule-making body. The Act also required that brokers and managing agents divest themselves of financial interests in each other within five years. The continued opposition of the large broking firms was tempered by their fear of stronger legislation and by the government's continued support for self-regulation.

16 BL C409/015, interview with Sir Peter Miller.

17 *House of Lords*Debates 1 April 1982, vol. 428, cc. 1472–533.

18 *House of Lords Debates* 1 April 1982, vol. 428, c. 1482 (Mishcon).

19 *House of Lords Debates* 1 April 1982, vol. 428, c. 1503–5 (Napier), 1521 (Fortescue).

20 Eliz. II (1982) chap. xiv (23 July 1982).

21 At the time of the Act, there were 3,794 working members in the market and 15,315 external 'non-working' members.

At the prompting of the Bank of England, Ian Hay Davison was appointed as the first salaried chief executive of Lloyd's in its history.[22] From the start, there was considerable suspicion among working members of the Council and in the Room about his role. Davison was chairman of the Accounting Standards Committee and had experience as a fraud investigator for the Department of Trade and Industry (DTI) in the 1970s. He regarded himself essentially as a trouble-shooter, tasked with developing better accounting rules, rooting out fraud and restoring Lloyd's public reputation. His belief was that greater transparency and the proper auditing of syndicates would allow Names to act as their own police force.[23] His time at Lloyd's, however, would prove to be far more difficult than he could have imagined.

[22] *The Times* 6 January 1983.

[23] Davison, *Lloyd's*, 6–7.

CHAPTER 6

The School for Scandals

Abstract Even before the Lloyd's Act of 1982 came into effect, several new scandals emerged, which were more substantial than anything hitherto experienced. These not only involved outright fraudulent activity, but also reckless underwriting, incompetent management and an absence of central systems at Lloyd's to monitor the risks taken by underwriters in the market. One major development was the growing number of Lloyd's members, all with unlimited liability, who fell victim to the frauds and suffered from devastating losses of their syndicates. Such members increasingly combined to launch group action law suits against both their syndicate managers and underwriters and against the Council of Lloyds. The scandals increased the pressure on legislators to question Lloyd's competence to regulate itself. The Conservative government, however, continued to support the principle of self-governance and Lloyd's remained outside the new regulatory authority introduced by the Financial Services Act of 1986.

Keywords Financial scandals · Fraud · Financial regulation · Solvency test · Disciplinary committees

R. Pearson, *Delusions of Competence*,
Palgrave Studies in Economic History,
https://doi.org/10.1007/978-3-030-94088-1_6

Even before the Lloyd's Act came into effect, several new scandals emerged, which together were more substantial and damaging than anything hitherto experienced. Early in 1982, Lloyd's were informed by Spicer & White, an underwriting agency offshoot of the large broking firm of Willis Faber, that there was a problem with one of the small marine syndicates that it managed, syndicate 895.[1] The syndicate's chief underwriter, Bryan Spencer, had exceeded his underwriting limits and run up huge losses. By the end of 1984, these amounted to £18m, or an average loss of over £25,000 for every £10,000 invested by its Names, who included the well-known British tennis players Virginia Wade and Mark Cox. The syndicate stopped underwriting in the summer of June 1982, but the extent of the loss was only discovered following its annual audit six months later. Spencer resigned before the audit, but the Names were only told of the deficit after the result of the audit was known. The problems, however, were apparently not a surprise to insiders at Lloyd's. Knowledgeable working Names had given syndicate 895 a wide berth. Of its 245 members, only ten were working Names and two of these were Spicer & White directors.

Although other scandals were far larger and more damaging to Lloyd's reputation (see below), attempts to address the losses through bad underwriting at syndicate 895, like those of Sasse syndicate 762, marked another step towards Lloyd's becoming entangled in sorting out the liabilities of delinquent syndicates. During 1983 and 1984, Names on syndicate 895 repeatedly complained to Lloyd's Council about the excessive overwriting, and about the 'incompetence' of the managing agents in dealing with the run-off of the accounts and their failure to protect Names' interests. They were also concerned that Willis Faber might be allowed to evade their responsibilities for their subsidiary Spicer & White.[2]

While Lloyd's began to earmark money from its Central Fund to assist struggling members of syndicate 895 to pass their annual solvency tests, Spicer & White, in an attempt to stave off litigation, offered the Names a zero-interest loan.[3] The offer was rejected and a writ was served

[1] The following paragraph is based on the account in *The Times* 28 March 1983.

[2] Committee meeting 20 February 1985, in Lloyd's, *Minutes of the Committee*, no.109.

[3] Committee meeting 10 April, 24 April 1985, in Lloyd's, *Minutes of the Committee*, no.109.

upon Spicer and White by some 170 Names, who demanded an interim payment of £3.5m to help them meet their Lloyd's solvency tests.[4] Spicer and White promptly resigned as the managing agents and were replaced by a new agency entitled Syndicate 895 (Run-off) Ltd (SRO), whose sole purpose was to manage the outstanding liabilities. The managers of the new agency, however, sought full indemnities from both Willis Faber and Lloyd's before they would commence operations, and this led to a long wrangle between the three parties. In the Council, there was considerable concern that an indemnity from Lloyd's would constitute an 'unwelcome precedent', though it was generally accepted that the alternatives, such as litigation by Names, were less desirable. Late in 1985, an agreement was finally reached, by which Willis Faber would provide an indemnity to SRO, while Lloyd's in turn guaranteed that the broking firm would abide by its indemnity. If it failed to do so, Lloyd's was to meet the costs involved and then recover those costs from Willis Faber.[5]

The syndicate 895 affair had not involved fraud, but rather reckless underwriting, incompetent management and an absence of central systems to monitor the risks taken by underwriters in the Room. The solution decided upon—the establishment of a new underwriting agency, backed by Lloyd's guarantees, to run off the outstanding liabilities—reinforced the precedent set in the Sasse affair of troubled syndicates being bailed out by the Corporation. In this way, the traditional principles of non-interference in the free market of Lloyd's and the unlimited liability of Names continued to be eroded.

In November 1983, the news reached the press that five more Lloyd's syndicates, writing aviation, marine and non-marine insurance, were in trouble.[6] All had been managed by the Oakeley Vaughan Underwriting Agency, which was owned by Spicer & White, the same firm involved in the syndicate 895 losses. Oakeley Vaughan had previously been the subject of a Lloyd's inquiry for writing 'tonner' policies in the 1970s, by which underwriters could gamble on the number of lives lost in aviation disasters, without policyholders having any insurable interest in the lives lost. Such policies had been regarded as a gruesome form of wager and as such unenforceable at law. They were finally banned by Lloyd's

[4] *The Guardian* 6 November 1985.

[5] Committee meeting 6 November 1985, in Lloyd's, *Minutes of the Committee*, no.109.

[6] *The Times* 3 November 1983.

in 1981.[7] Four of the five Oakeley Vaughan syndicates were taken over by the Robert Napier agency in January 1982, who knew that there had been some serious overwriting, but the 250 Names were not informed of the losses until the accounts for 1982 had been audited. Willis Faber, the owner of Spicer & White, refused to make any offer to the Oakeley Vaughan Names, at the same time it announced a huge jump in profits.[8] In 1985, Oakeley Vaughan was finally suspended from placing business at Lloyd's.[9] Some Oakeley Vaughan Names, however, unhappy at the continuing pressure on them to pay their liabilities, formed an action group to sue Lloyd's for failing to tell them of an unfavourable internal report into their syndicates and allowing bad underwriters to remain in business.[10] Several such attempts were blocked by US judges, who ruled that they had no power to pass judgement on the matter.[11] In 1992, an action claiming negligence, brought to the High Court in London by 33 Names who suffered losses of over £5m, was dismissed when the judge ruled that Lloyd's did not owe a duty of care to its members.[12]

The Oakeley Vaughan losses, like those of syndicate 895, were the result of bad underwriting, inadequate monitoring and incompetent management, but unlike syndicate 895, they did lead to litigation directly against Lloyd's by disgruntled Names. In this respect, the Oakeley Vaughan affair was typical of a trend of the later 1980s, which saw Lloyd's battling against an ever growing army of litigious and angry Names who had suffered in a similar way. Other scandals involved outright frauds, though it is an open question whether reckless underwriting and fraudulent underwriting, both being driven by greed and facilitated by incompetent management, were qualitatively different phenomena.[13] A fraudster who is caught might be also deemed reckless, incompetent and negligent of his own long-run welfare, let alone that of others. Certainly,

[7] *The Times* 9 June 1981.

[8] *The Guardian* 21 March 1985.

[9] At the same time, a new agency company, Lionworld, was also formed to take over the run-off operations from Robert Napier. Committee meetings 1 May, 8 May, 27 November 1985, in Lloyd's, *Minutes of the Committee*, no. 109.

[10] *The Economist* 27 July 1991.

[11] *The Guardian* 3 September 1991.

[12] *The Guardian* 3 July, 30 July 1992; *The Economist* 4 July 1992.

[13] 'Greed was the root cause of the majority of scandals and problems that Lloyd's has had in the last 15 years...', BL C409/027, interview with Terence Higgins, dated 1989.

this accusation could be levied against the biggest financial crooks of the era, such as Bernie Madoff, no matter how long a fraud remained undetected, the failure of detection also often resulting largely from the incompetence of others.[14] Legal scholars have noted how English law is much more developed in the area of agents' fiduciary duties than in the area of competence, and how financial crime has long tended to be categorised as something different and more ambiguous than 'ordinary' crime.[15] In the end, whether Lloyd's Names lost money, and sometimes everything they owned, through fraudulent or careless underwriting, mattered little to them. They sought redress from Lloyd's in their thousands.

One large fraud, in which several Lloyd's underwriters syphoned syndicate funds into their own pockets via an offshore reinsurance vehicle, was uncovered at the end of 1982, though the fraud had been running for over a decade by then. In 1971, two underwriters, Raymond Brooks and Terence Dooley, established the Fidentia Marine Insurance Company Ltd, registered in Bermuda with a share capital of £12,500. In the following six years, Fidentia's capital soared to £1.25m, largely through the capitalization of profits. Fidentia grew so quickly in large part due to advantageous reinsurance contracts being placed with it by several Lloyd's broking firms, most notably Bellew, Parry & Raven (BPR), whose directors also had interests in Fidentia. Risks insured by Brooks and Dooley on behalf of eight of their syndicates were in turn reinsured with companies located in offshore tax havens, most often Fidentia, but also other companies in Bermuda and the Cayman Islands, who in turn would pass on the reinsurances to Fidentia. One feature of these contracts was that only one reinsurer was named, whereas normally a large number of companies would appear in a reinsurance contract, each taking a proportion of the risk. Another feature was the huge premiums paid out for the reinsurance as a proportion of the sums reinsured. These amounted to as much as 50% on some contracts, compared to around 10% for normal reinsurances. A third unusual feature of the Brooks-Dooley contracts was the stipulation that the premiums paid to the reinsurance company should be retained by it for eight years, rather than the normal three, after which a proportion

[14] Henriques, *Bernie Madoff*.

[15] My thanks to Sarah Wilson for this point. See Wilson, *Financial Crime*, 18–24, 42–4, 74–5.

of the premium would be returned to the first insurer (in this case the Brooks-Dooley syndicates) if claims on the policy had not been substantial. This allowed the reinsurers, Fidentia, to invest and earn returns on the premiums for much longer than was usual in reinsurance contracts. It was estimated that over £12m in premiums was paid out either directly or indirectly to Fidentia by two of the Brooks-Dooley syndicates, before incriminating documents detailing the contracts were leaked to *The Times* in 1982.[16]

Under pressure from the press, a committee of inquiry into the Fidentia affair was appointed by the new Lloyd's Council early in 1983, and some members expressed the view that 'the Council should have been more involved with this matter'.[17] The Council considered suspending the two senior underwriters, Brooks and Dooley, at this stage but decided against this after they gave an undertaking to disclose full details of the assets of the companies involved in the affair. Once further information emerged from the investigation, however, Lloyd's suspended Brooks and Dooley.[18] In response, Brooks and Dooley took Lloyds to court claiming that they were immune from any disciplinary proceedings because the alleged offences took place before Lloyd's Act of 1982, and the new byelaws which followed, came into effect. Early in 1984, the High Court in London ruled against the two underwriters, judging that nothing in Lloyd's Act prevented it being applied to past events.[19] This was an important ruling for Lloyd's. If it had gone the other way, it would have effectively granted an amnesty to nearly all the growing number of members who were currently under investigation. At the end of the year, the Council resolved to exclude Brooks and Dooley from Lloyd's. Neither appealed their sentences, and Brooks did not even respond to Lloyd's letters. Dooley did submit written representations, and, although he admitted the charges of misconduct, he appeared in person before the Council to appeal for clemency on grounds of financial hardship, which may have helped reduce his punishment from exclusion to suspension.[20]

[16] *The Times* 10 December 1982.

[17] Council meetings 21 March, 18 April 1983, in Lloyd's, *Minutes of Council, no.1.*

[18] *The Times* 6 October 1983; Council meeting 24 October 1983, in Lloyd's, *Minutes of Council, no.1.*

[19] *The Times* 7 March 1984.

[20] Council meeting 10 December 1984, in Lloyd's, *Minutes of Council, no.1.*

This was not the end of the matter. The fall-out from the Fidentia affair continued into the late 1980s. A programme on Channel Four TV in April 1986 highlighted those involved from BPR who had yet to face charges, and the bad publicity caused further consternation at Lloyd's.[21] In the House of Commons, the Labour MP Brian Sedgemore called on the Conservative government to set up an inquiry into the activities of BPR, 'and the interests of its directors in overseas re-insurance companies with which their syndicates did business'.[22] A few months, Labour's Shadow Trade Secretary Bryan Gould, citing Fidentia and other scandals, moved an amendment to remove clause 40 from the new Financial Services bill, which excluded Lloyds from the bill's provision for a new regulatory body for the City. His frustration was evident for all to hear:

> It is right to ask how one licenses the reinsurers when they are set up offshore. How would that have been done in the Bellew Parry Raven case? Those companies were set up in Bermuda by Bermudan lawyers who were the directors and shareholders. It is virtually impossible. But those companies were founded in 1970 and it is now 1986 - 16 years on. My understanding is that Lloyd's has asked its solicitors to draw up charges against the people involved. It will be another two or three years before those charges have been heard. There will be an appeal and that will take another year. The papers may go to the Director of Public Prosecutions and we shall be in the 1990s before we know anything about what went on. What is the purpose of having a regulatory organisation when it can take 20 years before we can draw the appropriate lessons from what went on. Of course, it is nonsense. Of course, it is a scandal. Of course, it is unsatisfactory.[23]

Meanwhile, disciplinary proceedings were commenced by Lloyd' against four more individuals, including John Parry and Frederick Raven, with penalties of censure and reprimand recommended.[24] One defendant, B. C. Peers, asserted that his penalty of censure 'was unduly severe'. He had committed only 'errors of judgement'.

[21] Council meeting 14 April 1986, in Lloyd's, *Minutes of Council, no.2.*

[22] *House of Commons Debates* 8 April 1986, vol. 95, c. 23W (Sedgemore).

[23] *House of Commons Debates* 12 June 1986, vol. 99, cc. 577–8 (Gould).

[24] The following quotations derive from the account of the Special Council meeting 10 November 1986, in Lloyd's, *Minutes of Council, no.2.*

> He had entered Lloyd's 16 years ago at the age of 45 with no market experience. He queried whether he could have challenged as a middle-aged newcomer the practices of those with Mr Brooks' and Mr Dooley's experience.

In short, Peers' defence consisted of claiming that he was guilty only of too much deference to his seniors, rather than of an act committed for personal gain. Minor guilt through incompetence was a theme also taken up by the solicitor representing Parry and Raven, who argued that Lloyd's investigating committee had not found:

> …that his clients had actually appreciated that the terms of the reinsurance treaties were unjustified, but merely that they should have appreciated that they were.

His clients had been found guilty merely of '…a slight imbalance in the relationship between enterprise and observance of Lloyd's regulations, bearing in mind the period when these offences occurred'.

Lloyd's disciplinary proceedings against the three principals of the BPR firm, Parry, Raven and Arthur Grattan-Bellew were finally concluded in 1988, six years after the fraud was revealed, when all three were found guilty of 'dishonourable, discreditable and detrimental conduct' in cheating the Names of syndicates under their control, by filtering funds into offshore reinsurance companies in which they had an interest. All three were suspended permanently from Lloyd's and the evidence against them was passed to the Serious Fraud Office. A compensation package of £15m, most of which was to come from Grattan-Bellew, Parry, Raven and their offshore reinsurance companies, was agreed with the 3,000 Names on the Brooks-Dooley syndicates as redress for their losses.[25]

The Fidentia affair, as well as drawing further unwelcome attention from Parliament and the media, fully exposed the cumbersome and dilatory nature of Lloyd's new disciplinary procedures introduced following the Act of 1982. The procedure involved, first, a complaint or allegation being received by a senior executive of Lloyd's. Lloyd's Council would then appoint a committee to investigate the allegations. The accused

[25] *Journal of Commerce online*, 11 December 1988, www.joc.com/four-underwriters-suspended, accessed 3 August 2021. A fourth man, Edward Nelson, was suspended for two years for placing insurance for the Brooks-Dooley syndicates.

were permitted to produce evidence and defend themselves, in person and/or in writing, before the committee. The investigating committee then reported to the Lloyd's Committee (the working sub-committee of the Council). After considering the report, the Committee then made recommendations to Council either to dismiss the charges, or to impose a punishment, which could range from censure or public reprimand; temporary suspension; prohibition from underwriting at Lloyd's but not a full exclusion from membership; and full permanent exclusion. The accused were informed of the recommendations, and at this point, they had the right to appeal to Lloyd's Appeal Tribunal. The Council then had to call a special meeting to discuss the Committee's recommendations and any judgement of a Tribunal. At this final Council stage of the procedure, the accused, together with their lawyers, were once again invited to make written and/or oral representations in their defence, before the Council made its ultimate decision. As Fidentia, and other cases discussed below, demonstrated, this process could take several years, especially if the accused contested the charges and temporary suspensions had to be regularly renewed. If an external criminal investigation was launched at the same time by the Serious Fraud Office, the time frame could be even longer, thus extending Lloyd's exposure to reputational damage and accusations of ineffectiveness while cases remained unresolved and individuals remained unpunished.

By far, the two biggest frauds of the period, with the widest repercussions inside and outside Lloyd's, were those involving the Alexander Howden and PCW underwriting agencies. In 1982, the giant US broking firm, Alexander & Alexander, acquired the British underwriting agency, Alexander Howden. When the Americans looked at Howden's books, they discovered evidence of a massive fraud and, as required under Federal law, they reported it to the US Securities and Exchange Commission (SEC). The chief underwriter of the Alexander Howden agency, Ian 'Goldfinger' Posgate, together with four fellow Howden directors—the so-called 'Gang of Four': Kenneth Grob (soon nicknamed the 'Grobfather'), Ronald Comery, Allan Page and Jack Carpenter—was accused of false accounting and siphoning off for their own personal benefit some £40m from the syndicates that they ran.[26] Syndicate funds allegedly

[26] Ian Posgate (1932–2017) had been elected to the old Lloyd's Committee in 1982 on a ticket of 'free trade for underwriters', but members of the former Committee were automatically to sit on the new Council of January 1983 as part of the transition to

had been used to invest in companies that the directors controlled in Panama, Bermuda and Liechtenstein. Gifts of cash and paintings were dispensed to buy silence from those who knew about the dealings. Posgate was dismissed as underwriter for two of the Howden syndicates, and Alexander & Alexander commenced a law suit against him and the four other Howden directors for £32m.[27]

Lloyd's Council, of which Posgate was still a member, was slow to react. When interviewed by *The Times* in October 1982 about the breaking scandal, the chairman, Peter Green, declared that problems at Lloyd's were 'no greater than running a butcher's shop'. When asked if he was concerned that much of Lloyd's insurance was reinsured in countries where there were no regulatory controls over reinsurance, Green responded by drawing on the old adage that Lloyd's was, and should continue to be, a free market:

> Let's get this quite clear. If you insure with Lloyd's, you have a contract with a Lloyd's underwriter. If he wants to do reinsurance that is his affair. It is nothing to do with you the policyholder. The Lloyd's underwriter places his reinsurance where he thinks it is best, where he gets the best protection, the best price. The responsibility for that decision rests fairly and squarely on the Lloyd's underwriter who is doing the reinsuring. He in turn is not interested where those people are reinsuring.[28]

The obvious fallacy of Green's argument was policyholders did indeed have an interest in the creditability and trustworthiness of the ultimate reinsurer of their policies, and by extension, this should also have been of concern to Lloyd's.

It was also obvious to many observers that the Howden fraud had only been discovered because of the US rules under which Alexander &

the new governance regime under the Lloyd's Act. Posgate, 'an amazingly clever chap' according to George Nissen, Deputy Chairman of the London Stock Exchange, was reported to have annual earnings of £600,000. The marine syndicates that he operated for Howden were the largest and most successful at Lloyd's (see Chapter 5, p. 46). *The Times* 14 January 1982, 12 January 1983; BL C409/054, interview with George Nissen. Obituaries include *The Times* 3 August 2017, *The Telegraph* 12 July 2017, *The Insurance Post* 14 July 2017.

27 *The Times* 24 September, 9 October 1982.

28 *The Times* 12 October 1982.

Alexander operated, namely that any company taken over by a US corporation had to be audited, either before or after the takeover, and the audit results reported to the SEC. As contemporary observers pointed out, there was an irony in the fact that the Federal financial supervisory system, decried by Lloyd's as inappropriate for the UK, was responsible for revealing fraud that Lloyd's own system of self-regulation had failed to uncover.[29] At the end of 1982, it was claimed in the House of Commons that the scandal demonstrated 'that self-regulation by Lloyd's cannot be allowed to continue', and that supervision of Lloyd's by the Department of Trade 'had not been good enough'.[30] The Minister of Trade, Dr Gerard Vaughan, was pressed by several Labour MPs to set up an inquiry into the reinsurance practices used by Lloyd's underwriters or to appoint a 'roving inspector to assist in the proper regulation of the insurance markets including Lloyd's'. Neither suggestion found any favour with Vaughan. The inaction of Lloyd's Council was castigated by one of his own MPs, Jonathan Aitken, who argued that it was 'essential to restore confidence in Lloyd's by putting an end to the present shambolic atmosphere of leaks, rows and scandals'.[31] The Labour backbencher, Bob Cryer, claimed the Conservative government was operating 'double standards', on the one hand restricting Trade Unions through aggressive legislation, while on the other hand 'refusing to have any sort of regulatory device over Lloyd's, largely because about 100 Conservative Members are members of Lloyd's. Scandal after scandal breaks out in Lloyd's, yet very little is done'. This was an early parliamentary volley in what became in a few years a deafening barrage of cross-bench attacks.[32]

Only after such concerns were raised in Parliament, and after the Department of Trade and Industry had launched an investigation and the police were brought in, was Posgate suspended by Lloyd's and an

[29] Davison, *Lloyd's*, 4.

[30] *House of Commons Debates* 8 November 1982, vol. 31, cc. 304–5 (Lofthouse, Moate, Fraser), c. 21W (Lofthouse).

[31] Aitken was a Name who had lost money in the Savonita fraud of 1977. See Chapter 4, p. 38.

[32] *House of Commons Debates 8* November 1982, vol. 31, c. 26 (Meacher), 1 December 1982, vol. 33, c. 200W (Vaughan), 6 December 1982, vol. 33, cc. 581–3 (Meacher, Aitken, Cryer).

internal inquiry appointed into the allegations of 'serious misconduct'.[33] A few awkward months passed while Posgate continued to attend Council meetings, but had to leave the room every time the disciplinary procedures relating to him were discussed.[34] Posgate did not go away quietly. He declared that he had been elected by the members of Lloyd's and not by the members of the Council, that he was in no position to abscond with funds, and that, as a member of Lloyd's for 36 years, 'he must have a contribution to make'.[35] He issued a writ in the US against Alexander & Alexander claiming wrongful dismissal.[36] He obtained a judgement from the High Court in London that Lloyd's had no power to suspend him indefinitely, though the court also ruled that Lloyd's could suspend all underwriting by Posgate's syndicates until the investigation was completed. Consequently, Lloyd's was able only to suspend Posgate for six months at a time, with each temporary suspension being contested by him through the courts when it came up for renewal.[37] Lloyd's Council responded by passing introducing several byelaws clarifying its right to suspend members under its new Act. The internal Lloyd's report on the Howden scandal, which eventually ran to 500 pages, was delayed as the inquiry widened to explore allegations that a further £500,000 had been channelled from a Howden syndicate direct to a bank account of a Lloyd's underwriter.[38]

Finally, in 1985, the disciplinary committee investigating the affair forwarded its findings to the Council. Posgate was acquitted of the charge of misappropriating funds, but found guilty of 'discreditable conduct' and 'negligence' in the handling of reinsurance transactions for his syndicates, and of improperly receiving a Picasso painting and a 10% stake in

[33] Council meeting 5 January 1983, in Lloyd's, *Minutes of Council, no.1*; *The Times* 10 December 1982.

[34] Council meetings 17 January, 7 February, 21 February, 7 March 1983, in Lloyd's, *Minutes of Council, no.1.*

[35] Council meeting 7 March 1983, in Lloyd's, *Minutes of Council, no.1.*

[36] *The Times* 27 January 1983.

[37] The duelling between Lloyd's and Posgate can be followed in *The Times* 12 January, 27 January, 7 February, 8 February, 1 March, 22 March, 15 December 1983. For the repeated suspensions, see Council meetings 21 March, 4 July, 5 December, 19 December 1983, 18 June 1984, in Lloyd's, *Minutes of Council, no.1.*

[38] *The Times* 22 October, 15 December 1983; Council meeting 5 December 1983, in Lloyd's, *Minutes of Council, no.1.*

a Swiss bank, the Banque du Rhône, knowing that it was meant to influence his underwriting in favour of the offshore reinsurance companies owned by the Howden directors. A note had been found from Posgate to Kenneth Grob, one of the 'Gang of Four', asking for the painting. Posgate, though he admitted negligent underwriting, was unrepentant. The note, he claimed, was just a 'facetious remark with no serious intent'. Lloyd's counsel, Peter Scott QC, however, argued that the gifts of the painting and shares in the Swiss bank were of a size, and given in circumstances, that meant they were not 'just the equivalent of a gold watch for services rendered'.[39]

Lloyd's Council held a special meeting in July that confirmed the disciplinary committee's recommendations of lifetime expulsions for Posgate, Grob, Comery, Carpenter and another Howden director, Mario Benbassat.[40] Other defendants received a penalty of censure, such as Gordon Pope, a Howden director, who had failed to disclose a gift of shares in the firm from its chairman, Kenneth Grob, which Pope proceeded to sell for £17,000.[41] Most accepted their punishment, though complaining of financial hardship with regard to the fines and awards of cost imposed. Posgate, however, appealed to the Lloyd's Appeal Tribunal, which substituted the penalty of expulsion with yet another temporary suspension.

Shortly afterwards, Lloyd's Council received an application from a new firm, R.L. Glover & Co (Underwriting Agents) Ltd, to register as a Lloyd's underwriting agency, with Ian Posgate named as a shareholder, a director and the chief underwriter. A member of the Council, Baillieu, admitted that he had been informally offered the posts of chairman of the new agency firm, and a non-executive directorship of Posgate's own

[39] *The Guardian* 13 February, 10 May 1985.

[40] Special Council meeting 8 July 1985, in Lloyd's, *Minutes of Council, no.2.* The scandal affected the health of several, though not all, of the accused. Comery died in 1986, Grob died in 1991. Mario Benbassat (1933–2011), managing director of the Banque du Rhône, became involved in running an asset management company, Genevalor Benbassat & Cie, that fed some $2bn into Bernie Madoff's infamous Ponzi scheme during the 1990s. Henriques, *Bernie Madoff*, 168; www.letemp.ch/economie/chasse-aux-millions-bernard-madoff, accessed 26 July 2021. In the case against Madoff, Benbassat was accused of receiving 'fees and/or distributions' to which he was not entitled. Securities Investor-Protection Corporation v Bernard L Madoff Investment Securities LLC, Amended Complaint, New York, 5 December 2010, 25–6.

[41] *The Guardian* 17 April 1985.

firm, Posgate & Denby (Agencies) Ltd, provided that the registration of Glover & Co with Posgate as underwriter was approved.[42] The application caused further consternation among the Council. Lloyd's chairman, Peter Miller advised that the central point was that a body should not be registered unless it satisfied Council that it was 'fit and proper'. 'When deciding this, consideration should *inter alia* be given to the individual and collective suitability of the board of directors and to the suitability of the active underwriter'.[43] Other Council members argued that

> the responsibilities of an underwriting agent are very serious, carrying the ability to commit a principal to unlimited liability. The fiduciary duties are based upon disclosure and honouring codes of conduct, and the question of 'suitability' should be considered against this background.

Concern was also expressed 'as to the truthfulness and willingness to behave at the margin of commercial propriety of the proposed active underwriter/director'. Lloyd's Council rejected the application, but Glover & Co appealed again and again, forcing Lloyd's to reject the application twice more. At the same time, Posgate continued to campaign for his return to Lloyd's, supported by powerful friends, such as Jeffery Archer, Deputy Chairman of the Conservative party.[44] Eventually, the reputation of Posgate & Denby was so damaged that it could no longer obtain the E&O insurance cover required to underwrite at all. Following evidence of serious overwriting by the syndicate that Posgate & Denby managed, Lloyd's instructed it to cease accepting insurance business.[45]

In 1986, two more Howden directors, M. J. A. Glover and C. L. R. Hart, both lesser culprits, faced disciplinary hearings before Lloyd's Council. The same sorry pattern was followed as that of previous defendants: guilt was acknowledged, but little contrition shown, let alone sympathy for Names whose funds had been stolen; others, notably Kenneth Grob, were blamed for the misdeeds; indignation was expressed at the fines and awards of costs; and financial hardship was pleaded,

[42] Committee meeting 24 July 1985, in Lloyd's, *Minutes of the Committee*, no.109; Council meeting 14 October 1985, in Lloyd's, *Minutes of Council, no.2.*

[43] Council meeting 11 November 1985, in Lloyd's, *Minutes of Council, no.2.*

[44] Council meetings 9 December 1985, 13 January, 10 February, 10 March 1986, in Lloyd's, *Minutes of Council, no.2*; *The Guardian* 15 January 1986.

[45] Council meeting 9 June 1986, in Lloyd's, *Minutes of Council, no.2.*

accompanied by a large serving of self-pity. Colin Hart felt that 'as someone of 30 years standing in Lloyd's, he would receive more understanding from the Council'. Despite calls by some Council members for greater leniency, the majority were in no mood for this. Hart was excluded from Lloyd's membership, permanently suspended from the right to transact insurance business there, fined £175,000 and required to pay £80,000 towards Lloyd's costs. Glover received a censure and was required to pay £14,250 towards Lloyd's legal costs.[46]

In the meantime, the DTI investigation into the Howden scandal that had begun late in 1982 continued. Kenneth Grob, who had dual Swiss-UK nationality, fled to Switzerland from where he could not be extradited. Finally, in 1988, the DTI's report, much delayed due to the difficult of collecting evidence, was published. It levied 72 charges against Ian Posgate, Colin Hart and the 'Gang of Four'. They were accused of theft and conspiracy to defraud Names and steal from the Howden syndicates. Grob alone was accused of stealing $1.136m. The DTI investigators concluded that the Swiss Banque du Rhône had been acquired with about $7m of syndicate money and that the culprits appeared to regard this as part of their personal property. Not only had the accused plundered the syndicates to bolster their own wealth, but they had also operated a complex scheme to inflate the profits of their insurance broking company. Grob had been keen to maintain the appearance of growing profits to help support the status of his company, and hence his personal prestige.[47] Two of those investigated were not prosecuted. Ronald Comery had died two years earlier, and the charges against Howden's former finance director, Allan Page, were dropped after he was certified as being seriously ill with 'a short life expectation'. Posgate, Grob, Carpenter and Hart pleaded not guilty and were committed for trial, but in 1989 they were acquitted on grounds of insufficient evidence. After seven years, this marked the end of the disciplinary and legal proceedings arising out of the Howden fraud, though the financial losses continued to reverberate. Most of the missing £45m had to be met out of the general funds of Lloyd's membership, just £13m was recovered from the assets of Grob, Carpenter, Page

[46] Special Council meetings 14 July, 13 October 1986, in Lloyd's, *Minutes of Council, no.2.*

[47] *The Guardian* 30 August 1990.

and Comery. Although acquitted of all criminal charges, Posgate never worked at Lloyd's again.[48]

Those managing Lloyd's expressed shock at the level of unscrupulous behaviour by 'Mr Grob's lot'.

> We got out the figures for the Howden Group and we found that as much premium was coming out as was going in - churning money. The reason was they own syndicates and force them to do reinsurances…which we now know to have been… the vehicle for theft of money from the Names…It was a hell of a shock for us…Lloyd's had bumbled along for years with immense success. We had always assumed…top brokers like Grob were men of personal honesty.[49]

Apart from having to try to replace the money stolen from the Howden syndicates, Lloyd's faced investigation by the Inland Revenue into the tax liability on various forms of reinsurance contract that featured in the scandal, such as rollover policies, time and distance policies, and reinsurance-to-close.[50] These contracts were hardly unique to Howden. When Lloyd's Council discussed the issue in 1985, only five of the 28 members of Council were able to declare that their syndicates had no interest in any of those types of reinsurance. After protracted negotiations, Lloyd's was finally able to settle the tax bill for a payment of £43m, drawn from money borrowed against Lloyd's assets.[51]

An even larger fraud involved the syndicates managed by the PCW underwriting agency, which was owned by the large broking firm Minet. John Wallrock, Minet's chairman, resigned in 1982 after it was discovered that he and several PCW executives had personally benefitted from reinsurances made by the syndicates. PCW, its manager Peter Dixon and the chief underwriter, Peter Cameron-Webb, were investigated by both the DTI and Lloyd's.[52] The auditors Price Waterhouse found PCW accounts

[48] *The Guardian* 19 May, 5 August 1987, 7 June, 3 September 1988, 30 August 1990.

[49] BL C409/015, interview with Peter Miller.

[50] For definitions of these contracts, see Glossary.

[51] Council meeting 14 October 1985, in Lloyd's, *Minutes of Council, no.2*; *The Guardian* 15 October 1985. It was claimed that 79 syndicates held time and distance policies, and that these were 'an excuse for inadequate reserving'. *The Guardian* 4 September 1989.

[52] Council meeting 21 March 1983, in Lloyd's, *Minutes of Council, no.1*; *The Times* 21 April, 9 August 1983; *The Guardian* 27 June 1985.

in 'an appalling state'.[53] Total losses incurred by the syndicates between 1979 and 1985 came to £235m. Most of the losses derived from poor underwriting, particularly from reinsuring US asbestos risks, rather than outright fraud. The total liability facing the 1,500 Names in the PCW syndicates came to £135m. For about 450 of these Names, the losses exceeded the assets they held on deposit at Lloyd's. Their aggregate deficit was over £15m.[54]

Once the fraud had been revealed and the magnitude of the losses were known, Lloyd's faced three urgent challenges: first, to enable as many PCW Names as possible to pass their solvency test, which would avoid Names being suspended from being in default; second, to find a way of funding the losses and paying the outstanding claims; third, to instigate disciplinary proceedings against the culprits. In July 1984, Lloyd's Council considered it 'of overriding importance' that the solvency test be completed for PCW Names 'in a timely manner', partly because of the knock-on effect on their other syndicates of large numbers of PCW Names defaulting, and partly because American Names had to comply with filing requirements in the State of New York, in order for Lloyd's to retain its right to transact business there. Lloyd's therefore quickly set aside £18.5m from its Central Fund to lend to Names who could not produce sufficient assets to meet their calls.[55] Complaints from PCW Names soon began to arrive at Lloyd's. A Names' action group was formed to resist calls and to pursue compensation.[56] Some sympathy was expressed by members of Lloyd's Council, who claimed that the underwriters and policyholder were innocent, and that it was the underwriting agent and broker 'who had not carried out their duties'. Council chairman Peter Miller, however, was less disposed to relieve the Names of their unlimited liabilities. 'Although there may be allegations of incompetence, the main thrust of the ... Names' objections relates to fraud'. He reminded his fellow Council members 'that the agent was the Name's

[53] *The Guardian* 16 July 1984.

[54] The deficits in the accounts of individual PCW Names ranged from £1,000 to £200,000. Figures from Council meetings 9 July, 18 July 1984 in Lloyd's, *Minutes of Council, no.1*; Special Council meeting 16 December 1986 in Lloyd's, *Minutes of Council, no.2*.

[55] Council meetings 9 July, 25 July 1984, in Lloyd's, *Minutes of Council, no.1.*

[56] *The Guardian* 14 May 1985; *The Times* 14 May, 18 May 1985.

agent, whether competent or not'.[57] In short, it was not Lloyd's corporate responsibility, but the Names' personal responsibility to judge the competence and honesty of their agents, and Lloyd's should not bail out Names, even if fraud is proven.

At the end of 1982, a new managing agency, Richard Beckett Underwriting Agencies Ltd (RBUA), had been appointed to replace PCW and manage the run-off of the outstanding PCW claims. RBUA soon lost the confidence of the Names, not least because of the lack of information being provided to them and their mounting liabilities as claims continued to pour in.[58] In the summer of 1985, Lloyd's Council finally took decisive action. RBUA was told to sell off 'healthy' former PCW marine syndicates and to hand over the business of running off the non-marine business to a new 'sub-agency' appointed by Lloyd's, entitled Additional Underwriting Agencies Ltd 3 (AUA3), the third such body established to manage syndicates in default, but by far the largest. Many on the Council were concerned that an 'unwelcome precedent' was being set with the increasing use of the 'AUA' structure to set up companies over which Lloyd's had no control, but whose legal expenses Lloyd's was expected to fund. It was a 'dangerous move' to intervene in the market in this way, because Lloyd's thereby 'makes itself a target for claims from all interested parties…'.[59] Nevertheless, organising the run-off of the liabilities of loss-making syndicates in this way was regarded as the least damaging solution in the face of growing numbers of discontented Names. Lloyd's also pressed the brokers Minet to contribute to the start-up and running costs of AUA3, threatening, successfully, to refuse to renew its license if it did not agree.[60]

An internal inquiry was established to investigate the 'mismanagement' of the syndicates by RBUA between December 1982 and June

[57] Council meeting 17 June 1985, in Lloyd's, *Minutes of Council, no.2.*

[58] Committee meeting 8 May 1985, in Lloyd's, *Minutes of the Committee*, no.109; Council meeting 13 May 1985, Special Council meeting 24 May 1985, in Lloyd's, *Minutes of Council, no.2.*

[59] Special Committee meeting 25 June 1985, in Lloyd's, *Minutes of the Committee*, no.109.

[60] Council meeting 8 July, 5 August, 11 November 1985, in Lloyd's, *Minutes of Council, no.2*; Committee meeting 18 December 1985, in Lloyd's, *Minutes of the Committee*, no.109.

1985.[61] Lloyd's was pushed towards this decision by the Department of Trade. It was advised that 'an internally organised inquiry would enable political questions about self-regulation to be more easily dealt with'.[62] Meanwhile, the criminal investigation launched by the DTI in 1982 continued, but with little to show for it. Sir Patrick Mayhew, the Solicitor General, said that the delay in the progress of the investigation had been caused by the failure to secure evidence which was admissible in an English court, and that 'insufficient evidence had been available to justify criminal proceedings or an application for extradition of any of the people involved'.[63] By this time, Peter Dixon had fled to Costa Rica and Peter Cameron-Webb to the United States. Opposition MPs and some Conservative backbenchers became increasingly frustrated and angry about the events at Lloyd's. Brian Sedgemore tabled a motion expressing this concern and accused Lloyd's former chairman, Sir Peter Green, who was a close friend of Dixon, of profiting from the PCW syndicates through payments to offshore reinsurance companies in the Cayman Islands and the Bahamas in which he had interests, an allegation that Green denied.[64] A Lloyd's investigation later found Green guilty on some of the charges and he was fined and censured, though not expelled, for discreditable conduct.[65] In the Commons, the Labour MP Austin Mitchell described Lloyd's as 'the school for scandals'.[66] Bryan Gould declared that 'there is little in Lloyd's recent history to inspire confidence…':

> It could be said that Lloyd's role in that (PCW) affair was to obstruct rather than to help investors...What went wrong at Lloyd's was not caused

[61] Special Council meeting 24 May 1985, Council meeting 26 June 1985, in Lloyd's, *Minutes of Council, no.2.*

[62] Council meeting 17 June 1985, in Lloyd's, *Minutes of Council, no.2.*

[63] *The Guardian* 26 November 1985.

[64] *The Guardian* 11 November 1985, 9 January 1986.

[65] *The Guardian* 7 May, 8 May 1987. Years later, Timothy Goodwin-Self, Peter Dixon's personal assistant, testified that he was in the PCW offices one day in May/June 1983 when he came across three women shredding what they claimed to be Peter Green's 'personal documents'. Goodwin-Self could think of 'no valid reason' why papers belonging to the chairman of Lloyd's should be brought to the PCW office for shredding. *Lloyd's v Jaffray*, 153.

[66] *House of Commons Debates* 14 January 1986, vol. 89, cc. 974 (Mitchell). The allusion was to Richard Brinsley Sheridan's play, *The School for Scandal* (1777).

> by a few crooks at the margin. Those at the heart of the Lloyd's establishment embraced the ... reinsurance arrangements that were the vehicle for fraud. The regulators at Lloyd's lost sight of the distinction between what was acceptable and what was not.[67]

The Conservative government rejected Labour demands for prosecutions and tighter regulation of Lloyd's, responding that the matter was an internal affair.[68] Late in 1985, Lloyd's investigation reported that Dixon, 'a clever, dishonest, greedy and unscrupulous individual', had used a web of bogus reinsurance deals to channel PCW funds into his own offshore companies and other property. He had spent £6m on a villa in the south of France, £1.7m on investing in films, and had filched £1.6m as petty cash. Other monies went into a diamond syndicate, a Spanish orange juice company, a yacht, an aeroplane and real estate, all charged to the PCW syndicates.[69] Dixon was fined £1m and expelled from Lloyd's, although the fine and the costs of £215,430 awarded against him could not be collected as he was in Costa Rica. Five other defendants investigated by Lloyd's received a range of punishments from exclusion and suspension to reprimands. Three of them appeared in person before the Council, together with their lawyers, to plead their case. Most admitted guilt but, by railing against the scale of the inquiry and the penalties and amount of costs awarded against them, they did not appear to accept the seriousness of their actions. They focused primarily on the financial penalties they were required to pay and how impoverished they were. The plea of J. A. W. I. Hardman was typical of his fellow defendants:

> He knew that he would be found guilty on certain of the charges and he realised it was no excuse to say that he was simply an underwriter working for two people whom he admired. However, he too had been a victim in this affair and had and would continue to suffer great hardship as a result of it....[70]

[67] *House of Commons Debates* 14 January 1986, vol. 89, cc. 1009–10 (Gould).

[68] *The Guardian* 17 July, 29 July 1985; *House of Commons Debates* 16 July 1985, vol. 83, cc. 289–96.

[69] *The Guardian* 13 November 1985.

[70] Special Council meeting 11 November 1985, in Lloyd's, *Minutes of Council, no.2.*

In the summer of 1986, Lloyd's disciplinary process against John Wallrock and Peter Cameron-Webb came to an end. Both were expelled from Lloyd's, and they and Dixon were subsequently barred from acting as company directors.[71] Cameron-Webb had fled the country, but Wallrock appeared in person before Lloyd's Council to plead his case. In a lengthy statement, he claimed that he was unaware of, and not to blame for, the actions of Cameron-Webb and Dixon, and that the punishments were too severe. He denied that he had committed any fraud, complained that the scandal had wrecked his life, and that he had only kept silent about it to protect a member of his family with 'suicidal tendencies'. He admitted taking money out of premiums for his own use, but claimed that these were 'accommodations' that he later paid back:

> Mr Wallrock stated that he had been a devoted servant to Lloyd's all his life. As regards the 'PCW' affair he was absolutely distraught about the problems it had brought to Lloyd's and felt ashamed that he had not noticed that there was anything wrong at an earlier stage. However, he considered that there were many others who were better placed than himself to have known what was happening and they did nothing.[72]

Wallrock's plea to mitigate the punishment fell along the same lines as those of Hardman and others, but Lloyd's Council was in no mood to be lenient whether the culpability was one of fraud or incompetence. The damage that the scandal was causing to Lloyd's was too great, at the very time that the Corporation was desperately trying to keep itself free of the regulatory oversight threatened by the new Financial Services bill being debated in Parliament.

With losses mounting on the former PCW syndicates, a rising number of lawsuits being taken out by PCW Names, allegations that Lloyd's was in breach of the US Racketeer Influenced and Corrupt Organisations Act, increasing tensions between the Names and their new managing agency AUA3 as it tried to extract contributions to pay the losses, and the continued inability of AUA3 to produce any definitive figures for the individual liabilities of the Names, Lloyd's finally resolved to mutualise the losses through a 'group solvency plan', and, by extension, accept direct

[71] *The Guardian* 14 January, 17 July 1986. Cameron-Webb died in California in 2004.

[72] Special Council meeting 14 July 1986, in Lloyd's, *Minutes of Council, no.2.*

responsibility for claims by policyholders that could not be met by insolvent Names.[73] The plan was thrashed out at a six-hour special meeting of Council in December 1986. It involved a payment of £40m from the Names, or 30% of the total of £135m, as a 'just and proper contribution', with Lloyd's, Minet and several of the potential defendants in the scandal covering the rest. Lloyd's also agreed to indemnify AUA3 for legal costs relating to litigation by Names in the UK and US.[74]

An investigation of the PCW syndicate accounts by AUA3 revealed that many of the losses had been due to poor or incompetent underwriting rather than fraud. During the 1970s, the underwriters for the syndicates had written exceptionally large lines at low rates to obtain premium volume, and 'had acted as the Tesco of Lloyd's', while failing to obtain good quality, or any, reinsurance cover:

> (There was) no worthwhile reinsurance programme between 1972 and 1979 and where cover did exist the deductible was so large as to preclude recoveries. Furthermore, the quality of reinsurance left much to be desired.[75]

The AUA3 investigation revealed that Lloyd's faced problems in several directions in reaching a settlement with the PCW Names. First, there was the huge and unprecedented scale of the losses, eventually estimated at a gross £718m. Second, there was the inaccuracy of the estimates of losses, and as noted above, and the near impossibility of reaching auditable figures for the losses of individual syndicates, let alone individual Names. Third, the quality of the reinsurance cover was poor, estimating how much would be recovered from the reinsurers was difficult, and there was a high probability that not all reinsurers would pay up. Fourth, about one-third of the £180m estimated by AUA3 that should be recovered from reinsurers had been placed with other syndicates within the Lloyd's market, while the rest had been placed outside the market. That raised the possibility that the PCW losses would reverberate around Lloyd's and

[73] Council meetings 12 May, 9 June, 14 July 1986, in Lloyd's, *Minutes of Council, no.2.*

[74] Committee meeting 1 May 1985 in Lloyd's, *Minutes of the Committee*, no.109; Council meeting 13 May 1985, Special Council meeting 16 December 1986, in Lloyd's, *Minutes of Council, no.2.*

[75] Special Council meeting 16 December 1986, in Lloyd's, *Minutes of Council, no.2.*

affect other syndicates' results, in the same kind of spiral of concentrated liabilities that would explode in the LMX affair (see Chapter 7). Fifth, it proved almost impossible to segregate losses that were the result of fraud from those that derived from bad, negligent and incompetent underwriting. Sixth, as long as there was no settlement with the Names, there was a danger that litigation in the US would seriously damage, perhaps destroy, Lloyd's business position there, as state regulators delved into Lloyd's affairs and reviewed earlier judicial rulings that had benefitted Lloyd's American investors. Finally, Lloyd's also faced the difficulty of conveying to many of the Names that they were personally responsible for their gross liabilities.

The PCW affair provided further evidence that by 1986 the growing pressure from, on the one hand, litigious Names, and, on the other hand, press and Parliament, was forcing Lloyd's to traverse the divide between the ideology of Lloyd's as a society whose executive body only administered a market of free underwriters, and the reality that a growing number of people regarded Lloyd's as an organisation with a corporate duty to limit the liabilities of its investors, notwithstanding that there was no constitutional basis for such liability limitation. The settlement with PCW Names amounted to an admission of the reality and an abandonment of the ideology.

CHAPTER 7

Liability Crisis, LMX Spiral and Collapse

Abstract The largest and more damaging category of scandal at Lloyd's in the 1980s and early 1990s concerned the negligent or incompetent underwriting of 'excess of loss' (XL) reinsurance. XL policies involved the reinsurer agreeing to indemnify the first insurer in the event of the latter sustaining a loss in excess of a pre-determined figure that was the liability to be retained by the first insurer. The rapid expansion of the XL market at Lloyd's contributed to a growth in negligent or incompetent approaches to risk assessment. At the height of the crisis in 1991, some 20% of all members at Lloyd's had organised into action groups to sue their syndicates for losses due to poor XL and other forms of underwriting, and to pursue Lloyd's for compensation because of supervisory failures.

Keywords Excess of loss reinsurance · Asbestos risks · Run-off insurance · Catastrophe losses · Risk exposure

The Howden and PCW affairs were the most prominent of several scandals that centred on the fraudulent use of syndicate funds. An even larger and more damaging category of scandal concerned the negligent or incompetent underwriting of 'excess of loss' (XL) reinsurance. XL policies

R. Pearson, *Delusions of Competence*, Palgrave Studies in Economic History, https://doi.org/10.1007/978-3-030-94088-1_7

involved the reinsurer agreeing to indemnify the first insurer in the event of the latter sustaining a loss in excess of a pre-determined figure that was the liability to be retained by the first insurer. At the height of the crisis in 1991, some 20% of all Names at Lloyd's had organised into action groups to sue their syndicates for losses due to poor XL and other underwriting, and to pursue Lloyd's for compensation because of supervisory failures.[1]

The highest profile cases involved the Outhwaite, Feltrim and Gooda Walker syndicates. In 1980, Richard Outhwaite, a well-known marine underwriter with some 1,600 Names on his syndicate, was praised by Lloyd's chairman Peter Green for his work as a director of Lloyd's Additional Underwriting Agencies (no. 2), which had been set up by Lloyd's to manage the run-off of the Sasse Turnbull liabilities, and for 'looking after the interests of the Names'.[2] Just five years later, the 1982 accounts of Outhwaite's syndicate 317 had to be left open because of the scale of losses.[3] In 1988, a report was commissioned from City of London solicitors Freshfields into these and other losses. Outhwaite had written 31 'run-off' contracts that reinsured other syndicates against the risk of asbestos and pollution claims in the US. Some of the original policies reinsured dated back to the 1940s. The shortfall in Outhwaite Names' deposits was estimated to be £20,664 for every £10,000 that they had put up. Even more alarming was the fact that the ultimate scale of the losses was unknown for those accounting years that could not be closed: 'Members of open syndicates do not know whether they are sitting on a time bomb'.[4]

In 1990, a group of 865 Outhwaite Names, including the former British Prime Minister Edward Heath, the golfer Tony Jacklin, the tennis player Virginia Wade, the hotelier Rocco Forte and the publisher Robert Maxwell, sued their syndicate's managing agency, as well as 81 members' agents, alleging that Outhwaite had been negligent in writing non-marine asbestosis and pollution reinsurance. This was the largest legal action

[1] *The Economist* 29 June 1991.

[2] Notes of Proceedings at a General Meeting, 19 November 1980, in Lloyd's, *Minutes of the General Meeting*.

[3] Committee meeting 3 July 1985, in Lloyd's, *Minutes of the Committee*, no. 109.

[4] In another syndicate, C.J. Warrilow 553, the shortfall was estimated at £17,219 for every £10,000 deposited. In this case, 500 Names sued. By 1988, around 9,000 Names were linked to syndicates with large losses. *The Guardian* 17 June, 29 June 1988.

yet seen at Lloyd's.[5] Lloyd's investigated, but, finding no evidence of fraud, refused to take further action.[6] Yet claims continued to roll in on Outhwaite's 1982 account, so that it could not be closed. Facing an unprecedented wave of members defaulting on their liability to pay claims, Lloyd's established a Names' Hardship Committee, chaired by Dr Mary Archer, wife of the Deputy Chairman of the Conservative Party. Archer, who was a non-working member of Lloyd's Council, was clear about her task, namely to develop a systematic way of collecting bad debts, rather than to relieve Names in distress.[7] 'We're not an easy-terms committee', she told the press. 'I take the view that Lloyd's is not a place for widows and orphans'. Names who applied to Archer's Committee for relief were faced with 'a quite inquisitive questionnaire', as Archer herself described it. The leader of a group of Outhwaite Names complained that 'they want details of your spending, down to your daily purchases at the off-licence'. One applicant received 'a rather aggressive sort of letter' about his standard of living. One elderly woman was advised by the Committee to sell off two holiday cottages she owned, her only source of income.[8]

This was a much tougher approach to defaulting members than had been taken previously in the Sasse Turnbull, syndicate 895 or PCW scandals. By 1990, the scale of reinsurance losses flooding into the market was so great that Lloyd's felt that a harder line had to be adopted, but it fuelled rising conflict with the growing mass of desperate Names. By 1991, nearly 1,000 Names had joined the legal action against the managing agents of Outhwaite's syndicate, claiming £150m damages for the losses of over £263m that his 'reckless' underwriting had led to.[9] The managing agents were sued because they carried E&O insurance against which the compensation was sought.The trial, which began in October 1991 at the High Court in London, was seen as a test case for pending suits against other loss-making syndicates.[10] The court heard that

[5] *The Guardian* 23 February 1990.

[6] *The Guardian* 29 March, 8 October 1991, 13 January 1992.

[7] On Archer, see *Lloyd's Log*, August 1989: 5. She had been a Name since 1977. On her election to Council, see *The Guardian* 6 October 1987.

[8] *The Guardian* 21 July 1990.

[9] *The Economist* 15 February 1992.

[10] *The Guardian* 23 February 1990, 29 March, 3 September 1991; *The Economist* 19 October 1991.

Dick Outhwaite had been a successful marine underwriter, producing an average profit of ten per cent a year for his syndicates before 1982. Faith in his underwriting judgement was evident in the fact that some 500 of the 1,600 members of his syndicate for the year 1982 were working Names. Outhwaite's problems began late in 1981 when he wrote the risky reinsurance contracts, exposing his syndicate to unprecedented asbestosis and pollution claims from the US. The true extent of the problems did not begin to appear until 1987. The basic plank of Outhwaite's defence was that not even the most experienced underwriter could have predicted the unprecedented levels of asbestosis and environmental pollution claims that were to hit the London market.[11] However, the plaintiffs' principal expert witness, Ulrich Von Eicken, a former chief executive of Munich Re, declared that Outhwaite was living in 'cloud cuckoo land' when he wrote the reinsurance contracts.[12] The plaintiffs' barrister, Anthony Boswood QC, declared that US casualty business had long been recognised as a volatile area for insurers. Outhwaite knew 'virtually nothing' about this area of insurance, the premiums he had charged were too low, and he had failed to take into account the surge in asbestos-related injury claims in the US at the time he wrote the policies.[13]

> It is probably the case that never in the commercial history of the City of London has so much of other peoples' money been lost by the single-handed negligence of one Name.[14]

After four months, the Outhwaite Names settled out of court for £116m, mostly paid for by the E&O policies held by the members' and managing agents.[15] This was the largest lawsuit settlement in Lloyd's history, but it did not mark the end of the affair. A further court hearing was required to sort out disputes about how the compensation should be

[11] *The Guardian* 7 October 1991.

[12] *The Guardian* 13 January 1992.

[13] *The Economist* 19 October 1991.

[14] *The Guardian* 8 October 1991.

[15] Ironically, the E&O policies had been purchased from other Lloyd's syndicates, whose names included some of those involved in the Outhwaite suit, and who thus ended up paying for part of their own settlement. *The Economist* 15 February 1992; *The Guardian* 25 February 1992.

distributed.[16] A row broke out between those Outhwaite Names who had been involved in the legal action and over 600 who were not. Some of the latter rushed to join a further legal action to prevent Lloyd's from drawing on their deposits to meet claims.[17] When the E&O insurers began paying out the £116m to settle the negligence suit, they found it difficult to extract payments from their reinsurers.[18] Christopher Stockwell, the lawyer who was co-ordinating the Names' action groups, argued that litigating Names must be offered as much as they could expect to win in court, which he estimated could amount to £2.5bn. The maximum E&O insurance cover then available was less than £1bn, and much of that was proving hard to draw upon because it was reinsured outside Lloyd's. Stockwell's solution was for Lloyd's to borrow against future profits to pay the negligence claims, but he acknowledged that this might put off new members. Lloyd's new CEO, Peter Middleton, admitted in exasperation that 'almost everything that happens in this place has problems attached to it'.[19]

A second, even larger, case involving poor or incompetent reinsurance underwriting, concerned three syndicates managed by Feltrim Underwriting Agencies, who between 1987 and 1990 ran up £320m of losses on XL reinsurance of catastrophe risks, such as hurricane damage.[20] The average Feltrim name, who had committed personal assets of £30,000, faced a loss of £160,000. After he resigned, the chief underwriter, Patrick Feltrim Fagan, admitted that the reinsurances had been flawed, yet his auditors, Arthur Andersen, had signed off the accounts and new Names continued to be recruited through 1989.[21] Furthermore, Lloyd's had withdrawn £24m from the capital of the Feltrim syndicates to cover the liabilities of their predecessors dating back to 1983, leaving only £4m of reserves to meet the vast claims and to reinsure against future losses.[22]

16 *The Guardian* 1 May 1992.

17 *The Guardian* 10 February, 12 February 1992.

18 *The Economist* 21 November 1992.

19 *The Economist* 4 September 1993. Middleton, a former CEO of Thomas Cook, replaced Alan Lord as Lloyd's third CEO in August 1992. As a non-public school boy, raised in the north-east and a social-studies graduate of the University of Hull, he did not fit the usual Lloyd's mould (see above Chapter 3).

20 *The Economist* 26 January 1991.

21 *The Economist* 11 May 1991.

22 Southerst, 'Unnatural Disasters'.

Like their Outhwaite counterparts, many of the 1,700 Names in the Feltrim syndicates quickly reached for their lawyers. This became the largest single group ever to contest demands to pay up for the losses of the syndicates that they backed. Not only did they question the extent and nature of Feltrim's reinsurance programme, they challenged the role of Lloyd's in drawing funds from the syndicates' reserves, and Feltrim's relationship with Walsham Brothers, a Lloyd's brokerage, through whom Feltrim acquired some two-thirds of its business. In any other financial sector, such a concentration would cause alarm, but Walsham dominated Lloyd's XL market, taking a lucrative 10% commission on transactions. The Names also queried the roles played by Feltrim's auditors, Arthur Andersen, and by the 59 members' agents who continued to recruit to Feltrim syndicates long after news of the losses broke out.[23] A 70 strong group of Feltrim's Canadian Names brought a legal action against Lloyd's itself for failing to disclose material financial information to investors, neglecting to regulate and supervise its markets, and operating a market where cliques of favoured insiders reaped huge gains at the expense of trusting outside investors. The spokesperson for the group, Jacqueline Levin, had taken a share in the Feltrim syndicates, signing a letter of credit for £70,000. It was, she thought, a conservative investment. She alleged that Lloyd's had a responsibility to make sure that Feltrim revealed that it was a catastrophe insurer. Most Lloyd's investors were not knowledgeable about the operations of the insurance market, and the annual syndicate reports that they received disclosed little except an overall profit or loss figure. They gave no information about the risks underwritten. The Canadian Names claimed that Feltrim described its business as relatively safe 'excess of loss' marine reinsurance. 'It was presented like a mutual fund', Levin claimed, whereby the syndicate underwriter looked after the investment. In her investigation, Levin also found out that there had not been a level playing field. Many of the syndicates with the highest losses consistently contained the lowest proportion of 'working' Names among their membership. Only six per cent of Names on the Feltrim 540 syndicate, for example, were insiders, against a market average of 14%. The supposition was that the insiders knew to stay away from those syndicates heavily involved in catastrophe reinsurance.[24]

[23] *The Economist* 11 May 1991.

[24] Southerst, 'Unnatural Disasters'. For an admission that Lloyd's members' agents 'in the past…did not explain the implications of losses' to their Names, see *Lloyd's Log*,

By 1992, Lloyd's was working on a rescue package for the 'walking wounded', as the new Lloyd's Chairman, David Coleridge, termed the Names in default.[25] At the end of 1993, Lloyd's offered a joint settlement of £900m to nearly 20,000 Names across dozens of syndicates that were in default. For the Feltrim Names, this represented about 60p in the £. Lloyd's hoped that this offer would seduce the LMX Names, who accounted for nearly half the losses and whose negligence cases were rated as strong.[26] The offer was soon rejected by the Names' action groups, partly because its terms removed the right of Names to sue auditors or to refuse future cash calls. Until Lloyd's promised to cap their future liabilities, which had not been the case with the Outhwaite settlement, litigation by Names would continue.[27]

Running parallel with that of Feltrim, a third major scandal involved the syndicates managed by Anthony Gooda and Derek Walker, which lost more than $1.7bn in writing XL reinsurance.[28] The Serious Fraud Office began an investigation, but this was soon aborted for unknown reasons. Lloyd's removed the trading licenses of all the syndicates operated by the Gooda Walker (GW) agency and commissioned separate reports into this and the Feltrim case. Both reports reached the same conclusions: first, that members' agents had failed to look after their Names' interests; second, that managing agents were incompetent and uninformed; third, that the underwriters did not understand XL catastrophe reinsurance and had made a mess of it. The most serious charge was that insiders knew things were going wrong and took advantage of this by dumping their worst risks on to the stricken syndicates at absurdly low rates.[29] Following a pattern already set by Names in other syndicates, an affidavit was presented to the Commercial Court in London on behalf of over 800 GW Names in an attempt to stop Lloyd's from drawing on their deposits to pay for the outstanding losses. Lloyd's CEO, Alan Lord

December 1991: 6, letter from R.H. Passmore. For concern that some recruited Names to high-risk syndicates 'without a word of warning about their nature', see ibid., 6, letter from Brodie Lewis.

[25] *The Guardian* 1 May 1992.

[26] *The Economist* 11 December 1993.

[27] *The Economist* 22 January 1994.

[28] *The Guardian* 22 October 1991, 3 April, 6 April 1992.

[29] *The Economist* 17 October 1992.

admitted that the affidavit raised questions about 'whether the accounts of the syndicates from year to year were as informative as they might have been'.[30] In 1993, the administrators of GW revealed that staff-bonuses and company cars were being improperly charged to Names as late as 1991, shortly before the agency went bust. Early in 1994, the GW Names joined those on Feltrim and other syndicates in rejecting Lloyd's offer of £900m compensation. The House of Lords ruled that a 3,100-strong Names' action group could sue GW and 71 members' agents.[31] The Names alleged that the syndicates had appalling record-keeping and information systems and that they had displayed spectacular incompetence by breaching the cardinal principle that risks should be spread, not concentrated.[32]

During the trial in 1994, several GW underwriters testified that their directors had encouraged the losses to be covered up.[33] Anthony Willard, a former marine underwriter with GW, testified that:

> I was taking considerable stick from some fellow directors who suggested that, instead of telling the truth, I should be keeping quiet, putting my head down and writing more business.

Willard also claimed that Derek Walker and Anthony Gooda had suggested an insurance scheme to boost the apparent finances of the marine syndicate and disguise the type of insurance being written.[34]

Equally damaging was the evidence of incompetence that emerged at the trial. The expert witness Ulrich von Eicken, who had also testified at the Outhwaite trial, claimed that GW had failed to write a balanced book of business, had failed to calculate and reinsure their exposure, and had failed properly to rate the business they wrote. It was an 'aberration of catastrophe excess of loss business and should probably not have been

[30] *The Guardian* 3 April, 6 April 1992.

[31] *The Guardian* 13 April 1994.

[32] *The Economist* 30 April 1994. Some found it ironic that the Gooda Walker defence lawyers called in Richard Outhwaite as their expert witness.

[33] *The Guardian* 20 May 1994.

[34] *The Guardian* 20 May 1994.

touched by anybody'.[35] According to von Eicken, any competent underwriter would have written plans in advance of his aggregate limits, his estimates of the Probable Maximum Loss (PML), defined as the most serious catastrophic loss that could afflict the portfolio, and the reinsurance protection required. Other witnesses for the defence, however, such as Richard Outhwaite, testified that this was not how it was done at Lloyds in the 1980s or earlier. There was no formal planning, syndicates were run as ongoing concerns, and only if a syndicate changed its composition significantly from year to year, would an underwriter bother to plan his underwriting to accommodate these changes. The trial judge, Justice Phillips, agreed with von Eicken. It was a 'fundamental principle' of XL underwriting, he said, that an underwriter should formulate and follow a plan as to the amount of exposure his syndicate should carry. This required a proper monitoring of the business and making 'no radical departure from his policy on exposure so as to betray the reasonable expectations of his Names'.[36] Phillips concluded that one GW underwriter, Andrews, kept no record of his aggregate exposure and had no idea of how much this exposure increased as a result of major catastrophe losses. Andrews claimed that he regarded the total loss of a North Sea oil rig as unthinkable, and yet he accepted premiums to provide XL cover against that event. His failure adequately to assess and buy cover for his Names against such a loss amounted to negligence. It was clear to Phillips that Andrews never had a proper grasp of the XL business he was writing.[37]

The rapid expansion of the XL market at Lloyd's appears to have contributed to such negligent approaches to risk. Richard Outhwaite told the court that 52 of the 80 syndicates that commenced business between 1982 and 1988 wrote some XL reinsurance. Derek Walker had launched one of his GW syndicates, #290, in 1974 with 100 names. By 1989, he had 3,163 Names on the syndicate with a total underwriting capacity of £70m. Justice Phillips concluded that Walker had made no attempt to calculate the type and level of catastrophe that might cause a loss to his

[35] *The Economist* 8 October 1994. By a balanced book, von Eicken meant spreading risks and premiums over several classes of risk to limit exposure to a single event; estimating the PML; reinsuring up to the PML. This procedure, according to von Eicken, should be followed by reinsurance underwriters for each year of account.

[36] *Deeny v Gooda Walker Ltd*, 42–3.

[37] Ibid., 86–7.

Names. He had simply assumed that only the most extreme catastrophe would produce this result. Walker called his rating method a 'rate on line'. This involved assessing a risk over a period, as well as the client's claims history in respect of that particular account, and then assigning a rate to the risk. According to Phillips, Walker had:

> ...deliberately run a net exposure to risk without precisely calculating the level of that exposure or informing his Names. His rating was based not on any assessment of the earnings his syndicate needed to make in the good years to balance the losses in the bad, but on an acceptance of the structure and level of rates prevailing in the market.[38]

Here was a devastating and very public indictment of the way that the underwriting of XL reinsurance was conducted at Lloyd's. The GW underwriters had either not cared or not understood what they were doing, and had been keen to keep their practices hidden from scrutiny. The lawyer representing the Names declared that the underwriters had displayed 'spectacular incompetence' by breaching the cardinal principle of insurance, namely that risks should be spread, not concentrated. He invoked the image of gambling on the spin of a roulette wheel, with the difference that the Names never knew how much they had at stake.[39] In his ruling, Justice Phillips judged that the GW agency had been negligent when it exposed Names in five of its syndicates to huge catastrophe risks without adequately reinsuring them, that it owed a duty of care to all its Names, and that the members' agents were contractually liable to the Names for any failure to exercise reasonable skill and care on the part of GW as managing agents.[40]

The GW ruling paved the way for a huge compensation deal, one potentially worth £504m to Names, and set a disturbing precedent for pending cases in which other groups of Names were suing Lloyd's agencies.[41] As the sums suggest, this new generation of scandals was on a scale vastly greater than the earlier frauds. The scale derived from the large number of Names involved the long-tail nature of the asbestos and industrial pollution risks generating many of the losses, the enormous

[38] Ibid., 109–14.

[39] *The Economist* 30 April 1994.

[40] *Deeny v Gooda Walker Ltd.*

[41] *The Economist* 8 October 1994.

upsurge in catastrophe losses during the later 1980s, and the spiral of liabilities that the writing of XL reinsurance produced across the market (described below). Asbestosis and pollution claims in the US, which had concerned some at Lloyd's in the late 1960s, began to pour in, some on policies dating as far back as the 1930s. The risk of lung cancer continues to rise even 30 years after exposure to asbestos dust, hence the long gestation period of these liabilities.[42] By 1982, US asbestosis claims alone were estimated at $100bn. One US corporation, Manville, filed for bankruptcy because of many thousands of lawsuits and sought $5bn from its insurers, including some at Lloyd's, to meet the claims.[43] Following Manville's bankruptcy, the UK's biggest asbestos producer, Turner & Newell admitted that it was involved in about 1,000 asbestosis claims, though many were dismissed without payment and average settlements were small.[44] In contrast to the generosity of US courts, low levels of compensation paid to victims in the UK meant that as late as 1982 Turner & Newell did not bother to insure against asbestosis claims.[45]

These long-tail liabilities were compounded by an uptick in catastrophe losses, including the UK windstorms of 1987, the *Piper Alpha*

[42] For evidence that this concern was kept well hidden from newcomers entering the market, see "The Decline and Fall of Lloyds of London," *Time Europe Special Report*, 21 February 2000, www.time.com/time/europe/lloydsfile, accessed 10 June 2011; Luessenhop, *Risky Business*, 163–72. Asbestos cases comprised the majority of all personal injury product liability cases coming before US Federal courts between 1987 and 1991. Viscusi, 'Alternative Institutional Responses', 161–2. By the year 2000, the number of claims, including those settled, had reached 450,000. *Lloyd's v Jaffray*, 4.

[43] *The Times* 27 August 1982; Committee meeting 20 March 1985, in Lloyd's, *Minutes of the Committee,* no. 109. The leading Australian manufacturer of asbestos, James Hardie, experienced a sevenfold increase in legal actions 1983–89. Moerman et. al., 'Tale of Two Asbestos Giants'. For a positive retrospect on the impact of the asbestos 'mega-tort' on insurers' underwriting practices, see Stempel, 'Assessing the Coverage Carnage'.

[44] *The Times* 28 August 1982. Average Turner & Newell settlements were only £600 per claimant.

[45] The first inquest in the UK to cite asbestosis as a cause of death occurred in 1924. Turner & Newell established an asbestosis compensation fund for its workers in 1931, and the UK government launched a similar scheme that year in asbestos factories, though not in other workplaces where asbestos was in use, such as naval dockyards. Tweedale and Jeremy, 'Compensating the Workers'; Tweedale, *Magic Mineral*; Simpson, 'Unhealthy History'; Bartrip, 'Asbestos'.

oil platform explosion of 1988, the *Exxon Valdez* tanker spill and Hurricane Hugo in 1989 and the Gulf war of 1990–1991.[46] As new Names flooded into the market, underwriters increasingly competed for catastrophe business, and more syndicates like those of Outhwaite, GW and Feltrim wrote these risks in the form of XL reinsurance. As noted above, under these contracts, the reinsurer agreed to indemnify the reinsured in the event of the latter sustaining a loss in excess of a pre-determined figure, which was the liability to be retained by the reinsured. The reinsurer in turn usually retroceded some of the amount reinsured to another insurer. Many marine underwriters like Outhwaite went into this market seeking large volumes of premium income that they could not find in the marine market, even though they had no experience of reinsuring catastrophe risks or long-tail risks such as industrial pollution. Some syndicates doing XL reinsurance retroceded to other XL syndicates within Lloyd's, so that instead of the risks being dispersed, the classic function of reinsurance, they circulated again and again incestuously around the same market, becoming increasingly opaque and concentrated in a few syndicates. This became known as the infamous London Market Excess of Loss (LMX) spiral.[47]

A simplified graphic of the LMX spiral is shown in Fig. 7.1. XL reinsurance was placed in vertical layers, each with a different premium rate attached to it. One reinsurer would cover a layer of risk in excess of the first insurer's retention limit. A second reinsurer, the retrocessionary, would insure the next layer of risk, where claims exceeded the threshold provided by the first insurer's retention limit plus the first layer of reinsurance. Underwriters could also write 'stop-loss' policies for individual names on their syndicates to protect them against losses over a certain amount. A collection of stop-loss polices could also be reinsured and in turn retroceded by the reinsurer.[48]

[46] *The Guardian* 15 January, 21 January 1991.

[47] *Deeny v Gooda Walker Ltd*, 72–4. For a contemporary warning of the need for reinsurers to be more selective in writing XL catastrophe reinsurance, see *Lloyd's Log*, December 1990: 8. A full analysis of the spiral's impact on individual syndicates was given by the inquiry chaired by Sir David Walker, Lloyd's, *Walker Report*. The spiral has been modelled econometrically by Bain, 'Insurance Spirals'.

[48] Luessenhop, *Risky Business*, 128.

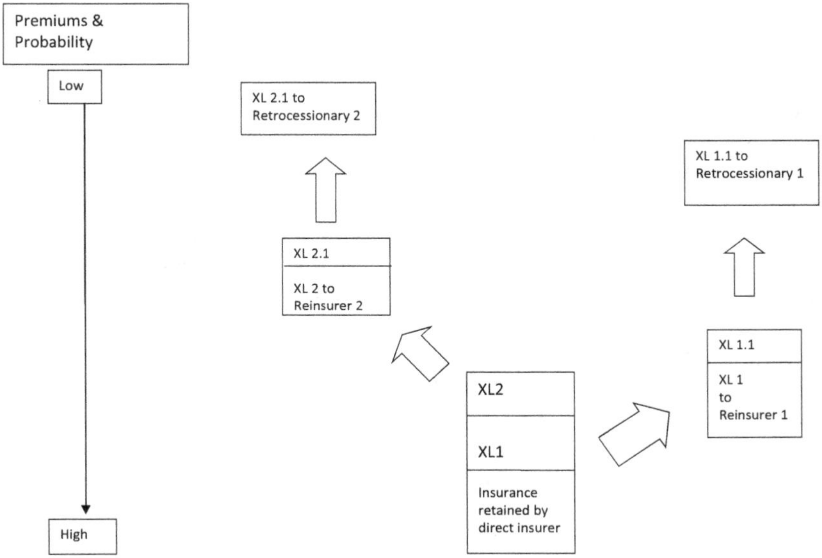

Fig. 7.1 Excess of loss reinsurance spiral

In theory, this process should have helped disperse risks by bringing in more insurers to provide cover. Because the probability of losses occurring in the upper layers of risk (XL 1.1 and 2.1 in Fig. 7.1) is lower, the administration costs and premiums charged for these upper layers are lower. However, when a loss occurred that was so big as to trigger the reinsurance on these higher layers of risk, the claims were often large in proportion to the premiums received. The defect at the core of the spiral developed when some syndicates writing XL reinsurance took out XL cover themselves. Those who reinsured them were therefore writing XL risk on XL risk. The latter, in turn, frequently also took out XL cover. Thus, there developed a spiral of mutual reinsurance. When a catastrophic loss occurred, claims were passed on, minus retentions, between syndicates in a complex game of pass the parcel. The first to exhaust their layers of XL reinsurance protection were left holding the liability parcel.

The effect was to magnify many times the volume of loss, because claims were repeatedly made in respect of the same loss.[49]

To illustrate this, consider an oil rig insured for £100m, but whose insurer only wishes to retain half of the risk, i.e. does not want to pay out more than £50m should a claim come in. This direct insurer therefore decides to reinsure the first £25m in excess of a loss of £50m (XL 1) with reinsurer 1. The second layer of risk above this, i.e. any loss between £75m and £100m (XL 2), is reinsured with reinsurer 2. The two reinsurers, for their part, only want to retain half of the layers of excess loss that they have accepted, so they retrocede £12.5m each to retrocessionaries 1 and 2, respectively (XL 1.1 and XL 2.1). If the oil rig catches fire and is only half destroyed, the total claim of £50m falls on the direct insurer, without a claim being made on either reinsurer. However, if the rig is entirely destroyed, the policyholder claims £100m from the direct insurer; the direct insurer claims the two £25m excess of loss risks (XL1 and XL2) reinsured with reinsurers 1 and 2; and the two reinsurers claim the £12.5m that they each retroceded from their retrocessionaries (XL 1.1 and XL 2.1). The gross claim, therefore, amounts to 175% (100 + 25 + 25 + 12.5 + 12.5) of the insured loss. Net claims, once finally settled, will come to 100% of the loss, but this shows how XL reinsurance could greatly inflate the volume of claims circulating during a settlement period, exacerbating liquidity concerns.[50]

The LMX spiral was kept turning by several factors. In the years before the huge syndicate losses, high returns enticed many into this business. XL premiums rose by 201% between 1983 and 1988 compared to a 61% increase for Lloyd's market as a whole.[51] By 1990, over one quarter of the business at Lloyd's was XL reinsurance. It had been just 13% in 1983.[52] Lloyd's own accounting rules encouraged XL business to be retained within the market, by crediting as reserves 100% of any reinsurance bought there, but only 80% of reinsurance bought outside the market.[53]

[49] *Deeny v Gooda Walker Ltd.*

[50] The total value of claims arising from the *Piper Alpha* disaster, including those on insurers, reinsurers and retrocedents, is said to have amounted to over ten times the insured loss. Lloyd's, *Walker Report*, para. 2.14.

[51] Ibid., paras. 2.10, 2.19.

[52] Ibid., para. 2.19.

[53] Luessenhop, *Risky Business*, 129.

As more capacity entered XL business, underwriters were encouraged to reinsure more and to keep their retention rates low. Lloyd's was later accused of failing properly to monitor syndicate underwriting capacity, the rates being charged or the provenance of the risks being insured. The spiral offered brokers, underwriters and managing agents commission and fees on every reinsurance and retrocession written, and in the wake of the losses, many Names accused their agents of gouging them in this way. Ian Posgate, the disgraced Lloyd's underwriter, told around 200 disgruntled Names at a meeting in 1992 that the LMX spiral was 'the City's version of pyramid selling', with 'clear advantages to agents and brokers whilst outside Names get hurt'.[54] Derek Walker earned £300,000 from GW syndicate 290, which made huge losses in 1989 and 1990. One of the key players in the LMX market, the broker Bill Brown, who accounted for 80% of Feltrim's reinsurance, reportedly earned an £8.1m salary from the Walsham Brothers broking firm owned by his family, plus another £1 million in dividends. Brown himself was also a Name, but only on top-performing syndicates, not on the foundering syndicates for which he was the broker.[55]

XL business also enabled underwriters to arbitrage by profiting from the differential between the premiums received for the insurance, and the lower premiums paid out for reinsurance and retrocessions. These opportunities multiplied where those writing at the top of the spiral accepted, out of ignorance or carelessness, premium rates that were far too low for the higher layers, believing that these layers were virtually risk free. Such arbitrage thus increased the moral hazard of underwriters insuring without much concern about their fiduciary obligations to their Names.[56]

XL reinsurance also offered a means by which unscrupulous underwriters could offload the worst risks onto 'dustbin' syndicates of outsider Names, while picking the best risks to be reinsured or retroceded with so-called 'baby' or 'preferred' syndicates of a small number of insiders, including brokers, underwriters, agents, Lloyd's executives and few favoured Names.[57] The problem of 'baby' syndicates had existed since

[54] *The Guardian* 25 February 1992.

[55] Southerst, 'Unnatural Disasters'; *The Economist* 31 August 1991.

[56] Luessenhop, *Risky Business*, 39, 64; Bain, 'Insurance Spirals', 15; Lloyd's, *Walker Report*, para. 2.20.

[57] *The Guardian* 14 February 1992; Luessenhop, *Risky Business*, 121–2, 154–5. For baby syndicates in the PCW scandal, see *The Guardian* 13 November 1985, and *House*

at least the early 1980s. Prime Minister Thatcher had raised the issue with the Council when she visited Lloyd's in 1985 and had received assurances that it was being dealt with.[58] It was still present, however, in the LMX crisis. Sir David Walker's Report of 1992 into the LMX spiral discovered that the syndicates with the lowest percentage of working names had the highest percentage of losses, indicating that a disproportionate share of losses had fallen on unsuspecting non-working names.[59]

Poor information recording exacerbated these principal-agent problems. Because of customary practice and the lack of filing space on the floor of Lloyd's, underwriters relied on brokers to maintain essential records, keeping only 'skeleton cards' with the barest details of what had been insured. The lack of a paper trail made it difficult to close the books on older syndicates or to track risks insured in the LMX spiral.[60] In his ruling in the GW trial, Justice Phillips noted that beyond the first layer of XL reinsurance, where the retrocessionary in theory could obtain information about the risk from the reinsurer, who in turn could get it from the direct insurer, the risk became 'totally opaque'. Phillips also observed that the LMX spiral concentrated losses on those who mostly did not intend to become, or even realise that they had become, the insurer of last resort.[61]

The Walker Report rightly pointed out that only a minority (87 out of around 400) of syndicates wrote significant amounts of XL reinsurance. Many syndicates that focused on other staple lines employed experienced and technically proficient underwriters who continued to insure cautiously and profitably throughout the period. Furthermore, the

of Commons Debates 16 July 1985 vol. 83, cc.289–96 (Gould). Even while these scandals were being investigated, Lloyd's Council decided against banning baby syndicates and opted for a voluntary code of practice, *The Guardian* 10 July 1985; Davison, *Lloyd's*, 144.

[58] NA PREM 19/1601, D.A. Dawkins to A. Turnbull, 25 January 1985; Andrew Turnbull to Maureen Dodsworth, 1 February 1985.

[59] Lloyd's, *Walker Report*, para. 5.16; Southerst, "Unnatural Disasters". It has been shown that syndicate profitability at Lloyd's between 1987 and 1992 was inversely related to the proportion of capital supplied by external Names. D'Arcy and Oh, 'Cascade Effect', 477. For further evidence of the skewed distribution of losses, see the data presented by the American Names Association on its website www.truthaboutlloyds.com.

[60] Luessenhop, *Risky Business*, 26–7, 48–9, 72.

[61] *Deeny v Gooda Walker Ltd*, 56–7.

heaviest XL losses were concentrated in just a dozen or so syndicates.[62] Nevertheless, these losses were so huge that they nearly brought down the whole market, especially when Lloyd's, in its desperation to meet claims, tried to mutualise the losses through market-wide levies to replenish its Central Fund.[63]

[62] Lloyd's, *Walker Report*, para. 2.1.

[63] All the LMX syndicates together accounted for over 60% of Lloyd's (negative) results in the accounting years 1988 and 1989. Lloyd's, *Walker Report*, para. 2.1.

CHAPTER 8

Reform, Survival and Recovery

Abstract By the late 1980s, while continuing to recruit large numbers of new members, Lloyd's was mounting an increasingly desperate resistance against external demands for further reforms to governance and business practices. The onset of five consecutive years of catastrophic losses, the growing scale of litigation by discontented members facing unlimited calls to pay for syndicate losses and the withdrawal of support for the principle of self-regulation by large sections of the British media and parliament pushed Lloyd's into making a series of fundamental reforms. Supervision of business practices was tightened and centralised, the outstanding liabilities from syndicates in trouble were detached from the rest of the Lloyd's market and run off through a new specialist reinsurance vehicle, and corporate members with limited liability were admitted for the first time. These measures enabled Lloyd's to survive, albeit in an entirely restructured form.

Keywords Financial regulation · Structural reform · Reinsurance to close · Group action law suits · Corporate membership

R. Pearson, *Delusions of Competence*, Palgrave Studies in Economic History, https://doi.org/10.1007/978-3-030-94088-1_8

While the LMX spiral was gaining momentum, new Names continued to flood into Lloyd's. Membership peaked at 33,532 in 1988, with new recruits still being attracted by the lower entry requirements, the tax incentives and the good returns shown by the majority of syndicates (see Fig. 4.1). Nevertheless, as we have seen in previous chapters, the pressure on Lloyd's had been building for several years. The overriding impression from reading the internal records of Lloyd's from the mid-1980s is of a circling of wagons and an increasingly desperate resistance mounted against the external forces calling for further changes to governance and business practices. In 1985 alone, for instance, Lloyd's Council was forced to hold a special meeting almost every month to deal with disciplinary issues. The chairman, Peter Miller, issued several strong reminders to members of the Council about the need to adhere to 'collective responsibility and confidentiality', to be on message when speaking to outsiders and to guard against leaking news about Lloyd's affairs to the press.[1] Lloyd's faced an ongoing wrangle with powerful brokers' firms objecting to the demand to give up their interests in underwriting managing agencies. There were protracted and 'embittered' struggles with the Inland Revenue over the latter's attempt to abolish the tax advantages of Lloyd's members' bonds and certain types of insurance contract such as 'rollover' policies, and over the Revenue's bill for unpaid taxes.[2] The Council faced demands to improve its systems for the disclosure of interests, to abolish 'baby' syndicates, to regulate underwriters through a code of conduct or a 'character and suitability test' and to control excessive underwriting beyond the premium capacity of syndicates.[3] It also had to address the problem of the evaporation of E&O cover for Lloyd's underwriters, as more and more scandals were uncovered.[4] Action groups of litigious Names on both sides of the Atlantic alleged incompetence by the Corporation in its failure to prevent fraud or negligent underwriting, and loudly

[1] Council meeting 14 January 1987, in Lloyd's, *Minutes of Council*, no. 3.

[2] On the disputes over the tax breaks for 'bond washing' and rollover policies, see Chapter 4, p. 35 and Chapter 6, p. 64.

[3] On baby syndicates, see Chapter 7, p. 87. For debates over codes of practice for underwriters and 'overwriting' beyond syndicate premium limits (a problem complicated by fluctuations in the £/$ exchange rate), see Committee meetings, 20 February, 3 April, 7 August 1985, in Lloyd's, *Minutes of the Committee*, no. 109; Council meeting 12 May 1986, in Lloyd's, *Minutes of Council*, no. 2.

[4] See Chapter 6, p. 62 and Chapter 7, pp. 76–7.

demanded that Lloyd's Central Fund pay the outstanding liabilities of the rapidly rising number of defaulting Names on loss-making syndicates.[5] On top of all these attacks from different directions, Lloyd's faced growing calls in the legislature and the media to dispense with the sacred principle of self-regulation.[6]

In November 1985, Lloyd's first CEO, Ian Hay Davison, resigned after a disagreement with Peter Miller, chair of Council, over what Davison perceived as attempts to restrict the independence of his role.[7] Relations between Davison and Miller and other Lloyd's insiders had deteriorated so much that Prime Minister Thatcher was warned to avoid the subject on her official visit there earlier that year.[8] Davison's resignation appeared to some outside Lloyd's to signal the inability of the Corporation to push forward with necessary reforms. Together with the ongoing scandals, it led to further questions in Parliament about Lloyd's ability to govern itself. In 1986, during the debates on the legislation to establish a new Financial Services Authority (FSA), Labour MPs demanded that Lloyd's be included in the bill.[9] The Thatcher government rejected this, arguing that the purpose of the FSA was to regulate investment not insurance, though it did announce an inquiry, to be chaired by Sir Patrick Neill, into Lloyd's governance.[10] This was dismissed by John Smith, Labour's Shadow Secretary of State for Trade and Industry, as a 'smokescreen'

[5] By December 1987, there were 76 syndicates with a total of 120 years of account left open, largely due to asbestos, pollution and other US liability risks. *Lloyd's v Jaffray*, 130.

[6] Committee meeting 12 June 1985, in Lloyd's, *Minutes of the Committee*, no. 109; Council meeting 17 June 1985, in Lloyd's, *Minutes of Council*, no. 2; Kellet, 'Regulation'.

[7] *The Times* 13 November 1985; *The Guardian* 12 November, 13 November, 20 December 1985; Davison, *Lloyd's*, 2, 34–5, 155–7, 165–6. Davison's resignation letter is reproduced in ibid., Appendix II. Years later, Miller continued to dislike Davison: '…he was not a man who could get on with other people…'. BL C409/015, interview with Peter Miller. See also BL C409/027, interview with Terence Higgins, for further negative remarks. Davison, however, was well regarded by the Bank of England and Whitehall as an effective and determined reformer who had done a 'first rate job' at Lloyd's. NA PREM 19/1601, D. A. Dawkins to Andrew Turnbull, 23 January 1985.

[8] NA PREM 19/1601, Maureen Dodsworth to Andrew Turnbull, 31 January 1985.

[9] *The Guardian* 11 January, 12 February 1986. See also Chapter 6, p. 55.

[10] *House of Commons Debates* 14 January 1986 vol. 89, c. 1015 (Howard). Neill was Vice-Chancellor of Oxford University and had chaired the Council for the Securities Industry from 1978 to 1985.

put up by his government counterpart, Leon Brittan, for not including Lloyd's in the new bill.

> Anyone who can speak so blandly about the merits of self-regulation, after having seen what some of these self-regulators have done in their own interests, is someone who is not taking a grip of the realities of the situation.[11]

The debates revealed that political alignments on the question of Lloyd's had begun to shift. Labour's front bench had moved decisively towards support for an independent regulatory body, though Liberal Democrats were not yet prepared to go this far.[12] Labour backbenchers attacked Lloyd's as a nest of corruption and called for state supervision. Many Conservative backbenchers remained in favour of self-regulation, but were increasingly worried about investor protection. Some were moving closer to Labour's position. The Bow Group of so-called 'Tory wets' called for Lloyd's to be brought in some manner under the auspices of the FSA.[13] The Conservative government, however, continued to support self-regulation, while outside Parliament, resistance to change came from Lloyd's Council, the large broking firms, 'traditionalists' and those wealthier Names who were best able to spread their investments around a range of syndicates.[14]

Aside from their attachment to free market dogma, there were possibly other less publicised reasons for the government's intransigence in the face of calls for Lloyd's to be regulated. It was well known that there were a large number of Names within the Conservative parliamentary party. As late as 1992, despite the exodus from Lloyd's having gained pace by then

[11] *House of Commons Debates* 14 January 1986 vol. 89, c. 949 (Smith).

[12] *House of Commons Debates* 12 June 1986 vol. 99, cc. 570–1 (Gould), 574–5 (Ashdown).

[13] *The Guardian* 28 July 1986. Patrick Jenkin, Conservative MP for Wanstead and Woodford, for instance, supported a statutory system of 'supervised self-regulation' for Lloyd's within the FSA. *House of Commons Debates* 14 January 1986 vol. 89, c. 968 (Jenkin). Officials at the Treasury were already discussing the virtues or otherwise of self-regulation as early as 1983. NA T450/349, A.C. Pirie to the Financial Secretary, 7 January 1983.

[14] On a private visit in 1991, Margaret Thatcher continued to praise Lloyd's as standing for the 'very best business ethics and the very highest of standards…', despite its appalling recent track record. Cited by Duguid, *On the Brink*, 72.

(see Fig. 4.1), there were still 62 Conservative ministers and MPs who were members, including four Cabinet ministers.[15] Government departments became increasingly exercised about the political damage that conflicts of interest might produce, if ministers became directly involved in regulating Lloyd's. The issue began with the Treasury, but it soon encompassed other government departments such as Employment, the Welsh Office, the DTI, Inland Revenue and Transport. The more this was mulled over, the more problems appeared to the Civil Service in terms of potential conflicts of interest, for example where a minister in charge of Agriculture and Fisheries was also a member of a Lloyd's syndicate that wrote livestock insurance. The obvious solution, however, namely for ministers to suspend or give up their activities at Lloyd's while in office, entailed costs that they were not prepared to shoulder, judging from the detailed calculations of potential losses that were made for each of these wealthy individuals. Between 1984 and 1987, two files of Treasury papers were filled with documents relating to this 'this tedious business', as one civil servant called it.[16] Various plans were suggested, such as requiring ministers to suspend active underwriting while in office, and placing their Lloyd's reserves and deposits in a tax-free account to earn interest. This interlocking of personal interests at ministerial level helped determine the Thatcher government's continued reluctance to abandon Lloyd's principle of self-governance, even after some Conservative backbenchers had begun to accept the need for external supervision. As late as 1995, the Conservative government under John Major declared that it was 'not persuaded that a change in statutory framework of regulation is necessary'.[17]

The Neill Committee reported in December 1986 and recommended increasing the representation of non-working names on Lloyd's Council to shift the balance of power away from the working members, but this was no solution to the tidal wave of insurance claims about to crash over

[15] *The Guardian* 14 February 1992.

[16] NA T364/509, P. E. Middleton to Clive Corlett, 27 January 1984. The files can found at NA T364/506, T364/509.

[17] Treasury and Civil Service Committee, *Fifth Special Report*, paras. I.13, I.25. The government did, however, promise to instigate a review of the Lloyd's statutory framework 'in due course'.

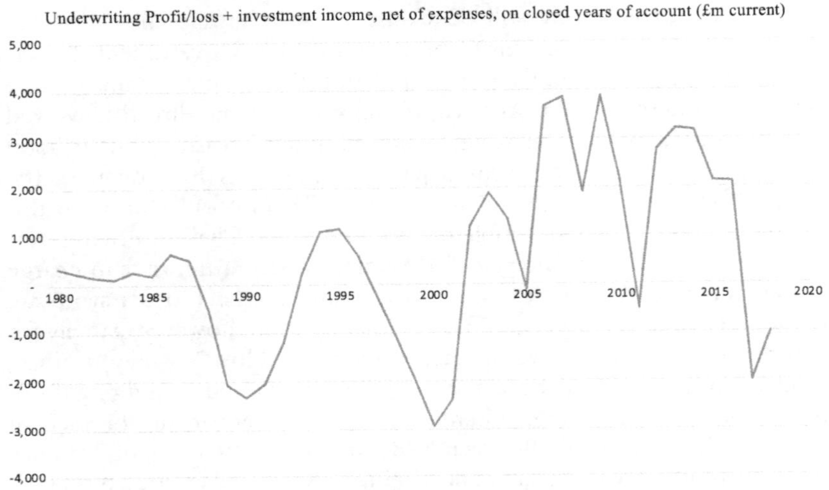

Fig. 8.1 Lloyd's overall results 1980–2018

the market.[18] In the early 1990s, after several years of record losses (see Fig. 8.1), the resistance to calls, and the lobbying and law suits, reached a crescendo. The most common grounds for legal action against the Corporation were that Names had been misled when they became members, and that Lloyd's had failed to disclose material financial information, had failed to supervise properly and had operated a market where insider cliques reaped huge rewards at the expense of outsider investors. As we have seen, in 1993, Lloyd's offered a settlement of £900m to the 20,000 Names on all the syndicates that by then were the object of suits.[19] The settlement was to be paid for by Lloyd's Central Fund, by E&O insurance and by contributions from agents and brokers. Set against total losses of £3.2 billion, it was not a generous offer—on average less than 30p in the pound—and Names would continue to be liable for future losses on past years of account.[20] Several action groups, such as Feltrim, rejected the

[18] Lloyd's, *Neill Report*. Davison believed that these reforms would provide the solution to the problems at Lloyd's. Davison, *Lloyd's*, 189–92.

[19] See Chapter 7, p. 79.

[20] *The Economist* 11 December 1993.

offer, partly because its conditions removed their right to sue auditors or to refuse future cash calls. Above all, Names desire some guaranteed cap on any future liability for losses.[21]

From 1991, the new Lloyd's chairman, David Coleridge, began to push through a series of measures, while remaining publicly optimistic about future profits, even though three of the worst years of account (1990–1992) remained open. A task force to examine structural reforms was established under David Rowland, later to be Coleridge's successor as chair of Council.[22] Two internal inquiries were commissioned, one to examine the LMX spiral, chaired by Sir David Walker, and the other to examine governance, chaired by Sir Jeremy Morse. Both reported in July 1992. Walker found no evidence of fraud but recommended a greater transparency of information and a tighter supervision of reinsurance.[23] Morse recommended a separation of regulatory and business functions in a smaller Lloyd's council, to be chaired by a salaried executive who was not active in the market.[24] Despite the opposition of most Names, a special levy across the market was also introduced to rescue Lloyd's 'lifeboat', its Central Fund, which had been drained by trying to cover the growing claims on syndicates whose Names resisted calls.[25] In 1993, in a breach of its own accounting procedures, some of the profits made that year were brought forward to replenish the fund further.[26]

The mid-1990s marked a critical transition for Lloyd's. As Fig. 4.1 shows, Names rushed to the exit door as losses continued to roll in. Lloyd's Council became more and more embroiled in a desperate struggle on several fronts, facing widespread resistance to calls, law suits brought

[21] *The Economist* 22 January 1994.

[22] Luessenhop, *Risky Business*, 254–64. Rowland was head of the giant Sedgwick broking firm and a member of Council. His nomination by Coleridge was denounced by angry names who demanded that the entire Council resign. *The Guardian* 28 July 1992.

[23] Lloyd's, *Walker Report*. See Chapter 7, pp. 87–8.

[24] *The Economist* 4 July, 25 July 1992.

[25] A Mori telephone poll of 459 Names, commissioned by Lloyd's in 1991, found that two-thirds opposed the idea of a central pool to bear a share of the losses made by syndicates with which members had no connection. *Lloyd's Log*, December 1991: 4–5.

[26] *The Guardian* 28 July 1992; *The Economist* 13 August 1994; Luessenhop, *Risky Business*, 254. Under Lloyd's three-year accounting system, the profits of 1993 were not due to be paid out until 1996.

by large groups of Names and claims that its preferential treatment of reinsurance bought inside the market breached EC competition rules. In dealing with distressed, rebellious and litigious Names, the Council adopted a carrot and stick approach, which combined promises of support to settle losses and vigorous pursuit of the assets of those who resisted calls.[27] The rejection of the settlement was quickly followed by the appointment of professional debt collectors and the establishment of a Financial Recoveries Department. In particular, Lloyd's tried to go after the awards made by courts to Names who had successfully sued. When the courts denied it the right to seize such awards, Lloyd's instructed members' agents to issues writs against their own Names on pain of being disqualified from the market.[28]

While continuing to defend self-regulation, Lloyd's pushed forward with fundamental reforms. The new CEO, Peter Middleton, introduced a business plan in 1993 that aimed to cut costs, raise standards, centralise some market functions and promote cooperation between managing agents, members' agents and brokers. A new Central Services Unit (CSU) was established to manage the deposits of the majority of Names and to act as members' agent to around 4,000 of them through a new Lloyd's Members Agency Services Ltd. The CSU was to process the data included in the annual statements of each Name's financial affairs at Lloyd's that were compiled by members' agents. It was also to handle all US$ premium trust fund accounts on behalf of Names and to manage UK tax processing for Names and the loss payments made to syndicates.[29]

In the same year, Rowland's task force reported and made two sweeping recommendations. The first, widely anticipated, was that insurance companies should be admitted to Lloyd's as corporate members with limited liability.[30] Limited liability had been discussed and rejected just five years earlier, when it was argued that it would 'effectively mean the end of Lloyd's as a distinct insurance market', and that it would destroy

[27] Coleridge had little sympathy for those in difficulty. He told a Name in 1994 that 'they went into a risk business, insurance isn't selling baked beans'. Cited by Luessenhop, *Risky Business*, 78. On the approach of Lloyd's Hardship Committee, see Chapter 7, pp. 74–5.

[28] Luessenhop, *Risky Business*, 280–300.

[29] Lloyd's, *Annual Report for 1994*.

[30] Cf. *The Economist* 26 January, 27 July 1991.

its competitiveness.[31] This argument was made even as the number of members leaving began to exceed those recruited and as there was mounting evidence of record losses on the 1988 account. The first corporate members joined in 1994, and they were soon permitted both to control managing agencies via holding companies and to put up the majority of the underwriting capacity of a syndicate. Some syndicates became wholly owned by a single insurance company, and there was a process of consolidation and decline in their total number.[32] Within a decade, corporate capital accounted for 90% of Lloyd's market capacity.[33] The old boys' club disappeared remarkably quickly.[34] The number of individual Names collapsed (see Fig. 4.1) and members' agencies all but disappeared. From a peak membership of 33,532 in 1988, there were just 773 individual members by 2010. Where there had been 270 members' agents in 1982, there were just three by 2013.[35]

The second Rowland recommendation, embedded in a scheme entitled Lloyd's Reconstruction and Renewal, was to detach the outstanding liabilities from the rest of the Lloyd's market, and run them off. A new vehicle was created, entitled Equitas and structured as a trust with a fund of £11bn, to 'reinsure to close' all non-life liabilities incurred by syndicates prior to 1993.[36] Underwriters, Names and their agents were to pay a reinsurance premium, in return for which Equitas agreed to process and pay any claims on the legacy business. In effect, Equitas was set up to function as a kind of 'old Lloyd's' comprised of all pre-1993 policies, which allowed the newly reconstructed Lloyd's to continue as an ongoing

[31] Council meeting 11 January 1989, in Lloyd's, *Minutes of Council*, no. 5.

[32] There were 400 syndicates in 1991, but just 62 by 2005. Swiss Re, *Sigma* no. 3 (2002): 20; Lloyd's, *Annual Report for 2005*.

[33] Calculated from Lloyd's, *Annual Report for 2006*. There were 95 corporate members of Lloyd's in 1994 and 895 by 2001. On this rapid growth, see Dilks, 'London Market'.

[34] Zinkewicz, 'London'. By 2012, only three per cent of capacity was still written on an unlimited liability basis. Duguid, *On the Brink*, 292.

[35] Duguid, *On the Brink*, 12. The 1988 total for Names is not that given by Duguid but the corrected figure reported to the Council meeting 5 April 1989, in Lloyd's, *Minutes of Council*, no. 5.

[36] *The Economist* 10 December 1994; Goddard, 'Lloyd's Profit'; Duguid, *On the Brink*, 279–80.

business.[37] By reinsuring to close in a single entity all the syndicates that had open accounts, it enabled the kind of broad mutualisation of losses that many at Lloyd's had resisted for years on ideological grounds. The Equitas project enabled Lloyd's, for the first time, to acquire information on the aggregate exposure of the Lloyd's market to over 5,000 individual reinsurance companies.[38] Moreover, Equitas not only reinsured to close all the open syndicates, but also reinsured the legacy liabilities of those syndicates that had already been able to reinsure to close their accounts, thereby releasing those liabilities from the books of active syndicates too.

Equitas did not provide 'finality'. If it was unable to find sufficient funds to pay valid claims, policyholders could still proceed with lawsuits against the original syndicates, and Names were still individually liable for any shortfall. Yet it became widely understood that, without the cooperation of Lloyd's, policyholders would find it almost impossible to collect from individual Names on old syndicates, many of whom were dead or scattered around the world, and that Lloyd's had done as much as it could to protect policyholders by creating Equitas and mutualising their losses in this way. In 1997, 95% of Lloyd's Names voted for the Reconstruction and Renewal scheme. Moreover, the de facto legal separation of liabilities through the run-off scheme finally became de jure when in 2009 the UK Courts permitted the transfer of syndicate liabilities without the acquiescence of policyholders and approved a deal between Equitas and Berkshire Hathaway which removed all remaining liabilities from the Lloyd's entity.[39]

Notwithstanding this progress in separating legacy risks from the rest of the Lloyd's market, it was clear to all sides that an agreement also had to be reached with the huge number of litigating Names. The pot of E&O insurance available in the Lloyd's market, standing at about £1bn in 1993, was too small to cover the compensation demanded by all litigants, but the cost of continuing to contest law suits over many

[37] Baker, 'Uncertainty> Risk': 74. I am most grateful to Tom Baker for providing me with a copy of his outstanding article on the insurance run-off market.

[38] Lloyd's, *Annual Report for 1994*.

[39] Baker, 'Uncertainty> Risk': 75–7. Lloyd's Reconstruction and Renewal paved the way for run-off transactions involving asbestos, pollution and health hazard liability risks to become a distinct sector of the insurance market, and for specialist run-off companies to emerge.

years presented a huge danger for Lloyd's.[40] After having several offers rejected, and after drawing on E&O policies, contributions from agents and levies on members, in 1996 Lloyd's finally achieved a £3.1 billion settlement with the great majority of litigants.[41] 1,752 Names, however, some five per cent of the total, rejected the settlement, and 216 of these pursued a further group action law suit, alleging that Lloyd's Corporation was guilty of fraudulently misrepresenting asbestos long-tail risks during the recruitment drive of the 1980s. The case came to trial in November 2000 when Mr Justice Cresswell found no evidence of misrepresentation or dishonesty by the Council and ruled in favour of Lloyd's.[42] This effectively marked the end of the mass litigation.[43]

In 1998, the new Labour government announced that Lloyd's would be independently regulated by the FSA, a reversal of the Conservative government's decision of 1986.[44] In 2002, in the midst of further heavy losses, an annual accounting system was adopted.[45] While these and other reforms were taking place, Lloyd's also became a more concentrated market, as mergers and acquisitions swept across UK insurance. Between 1991 and 2002, the number of brokers operating at Lloyd's fell from 244 to 126, managing agents from 151 to 49 and syndicates from 400 to 86. By the end of this period, the three largest broking firms accounted for 61% of Lloyd's business.[46]

Lloyd's emerged as a radically different organisation from its historical predecessor. Much market share had been lost, especially to corporate

[40] *The Guardian* 27 March 1993; *The Economist* 10 December 1994.

[41] Duguid, *On the Brink*, 281–8.

[42] *Lloyd's v Jaffray*, 5–6.

[43] There were several further law suits by Names claiming compensation for 'reckless' or 'unlawful' decision making by Lloyd's, but these also failed. In 2005, Justice Smith ruled that Names 'had no realistic prospect' of succeeding in their argument that Lloyd's was a public body and therefore liable for the tort of misfeasance in public office. *Lloyd's v Henderson*, paras. 70, 77.

[44] Duguid, *On the Brink*, 294–5. The FSA took over full regulatory oversight of Lloyd's in 2002.

[45] Losses included a record £2bn from the 9/11 terrorist attack on the World Trade Centre. *Financial Times* 11 April 2002.

[46] *Sigma* (2002), no. 3: 18.

insurers and brokers based in Bermuda.[47] Nevertheless, Lloyd's remained important in the markets it had long specialised in: reinsurance, aviation, offshore oil and gas rigs, and marine insurance.

[47] *Financial Times* 28 November 2001.

CHAPTER 9

Conclusions—Delusions of Competence

Abstract The history of Lloyd's between the 1970s and 1990s highlights the dangers that can be faced by complex financial systems from entrenched beliefs in the competence of experts and the efficacy of self-governance. The crisis involved more than contagious speculation, excessive catastrophe and liability losses, or a series of frauds. The reforms of the early 1980s may have temporarily alleviated some of the problems of malfeasance and misgovernment, but the underlying problem remained—namely an unwarranted faith in those involved in the process by which risks were insured and reinsured. Multiple delusions of competence were at work. Underwriters were deluded about their competence to assess categories of risk with which they were not familiar. Those governing Lloyd's were deluded about the competence of market practitioners and about their own competence to manage them. Legislators were deluded about the virtues of self-regulation and the competence of insider experts.

Keywords Tacit knowledge · Expert competence · Financial regulation · Ostrich effect · Cognitive dissonance

R. Pearson, *Delusions of Competence*,
Palgrave Studies in Economic History,
https://doi.org/10.1007/978-3-030-94088-1_9

Several factors brought Lloyd's to a tipping point at the end of the 1980s. Certainly, many of the inexperienced Names entering the market during this period exhibited signs of contagious behaviour.[1] One PCW victim told a reporter in 1985 that she had 'somehow got sucked into it'. She had been left £100,000 from her father and had been persuaded to join a syndicate by a Lloyd's agent to whom she had happened to sell a flat. 'They want £260,000 from me [in calls to meet losses]. I'm a secretary, I only earn £100 a week'.[2] More cynically, one might view the flood of new entrants as a manifestation of a culture of greed, in which the unwary were lured by ease of entry and by promises of tax advantages and high returns for little effort or risk.[3]

The crisis, however, involved more than a bubble of contagious speculation. A wave of catastrophe and liability losses far in excess of the normal underwriting cycle, tax changes, falling returns, scandals and frauds together made Lloyd's less attractive to unlimited liability investors by the early 1990s.[4] The failure of the governance reforms of 1981–1987 to be accompanied by revisions of operating procedures and underwriting practices indicated inertia, compounded by stubborn resistance by those whom Davison called the 'high Tories' in Council and in the Room to any proposals for radical change.[5] Reading the lengthy debates in Lloyd's Council and its committees over the content of the many new byelaws introduced after 1982, one has the strong impression of members digging in to protect existing practices, structures and power relations. If proposals seemed at all controversial or threatening, even where they were

[1] Gladwell claims that contagion is a function of social context and is one of the factors that lead to a tipping point in social and economic systems, an observation that appears pertinent to the crisis at Lloyd's. Gladwell, *Tipping Point*, 139–40, 158.

[2] *The Times* 14 May 1985.

[3] In the early 1980s, 73% of applicants were being accepted for the short so-called 'rota' admission interview at Lloyd's. Ninety-seven per cent of those interviewed were admitted. Calculated from Davison, *Lloyd's*, 224, no. 4. On the rota interview and the seduction of 'joining the club', see Chapter 3, p. 30 above; Luessenhop, *Risky Business*, 20–25, 32–3; Duguid, *On the Brink*, 14.

[4] By 1991, the top rate of UK personal income tax, which had reached 98% in the 1970s, had fallen to 40%, wiping out much of the tax advantage enjoyed earlier by Names. *The Economist* 9 March 1991.

[5] From a memorandum written by Davison in 1984, cited by Justice Cresswell in *Lloyd's v Jaffray*, 282.

the response to an external pressure for change, byelaws were repeatedly sent back for redrafting in order to remove the offending reform. Procrastination, rather than swift and decisive action, appears to have been the default position of many Council members. One example is the Multiple Syndicates byelaw of 1989, which aimed to remove conflicts of interest where an underwriter wrote the same lines of business for more than one syndicate. In 1985, the Rules Committee submitted to Council a draft code of practice that was, according to Davison, 'the end result of a long period of work', only for the Council to reject it and approve a byelaw that was hurriedly drafted, complete with typographical errors, during a break in the Council meeting.[6] Drafts of this byelaw were subsequently presented to the Council on five separate occasions, while members wrestled over the definition of offences that ought to be covered by the regulation, and worried that too clear a definition might 'open up a minefield for discontented Names who had suffered loss…'.[7]

Another example from 1989 is the Lloyd's Market Certificate Byelaw, which was drafted in response to a recommendation in the Neill Report of 1987 that all those intending to be active underwriters should be required to pass a new examination, more rigorous than the basic Lloyd's Introductory Test. Drafts of this byelaw were poured over by the Council for more than 18 months, while determined attempts were made to expand the classes of underwriters that could be exempted from the requirement, such as those aged over 30 and directors and partners of managing agencies, even though it was admitted that '…there was a general perception that the knowledge of some directors left much to be desired…'.[8]

With or without such procrastination, it is unlikely that these and the other governance reforms of the 1980s could have mitigated the effects of long-tail losses deriving from policies written decades earlier. Legal actions and political lobbying by Names heaped pressure on Lloyd's to accept structural reforms and to mutualise outstanding liabilities, while growing scepticism about self-regulation gradually pulled support from under the feet of the traditionalists. The political debates between 1981 and 1992 clearly reveal a shift in Parliament and the press towards an acceptance of

[6] Council meeting 9 December 1985, in Lloyd's, *Minutes of Council,* no. 2.

[7] Council meeting 10 May 1989, in Lloyd's, *Minutes of Council,* no. 5.

[8] Council meeting 1 March 1989, in Lloyd's, *Minutes of Council,* no. 5.

the need for independent statutory supervision. It took the confluence of these factors to transform Lloyd's.

Reformers, led by Ian Hay Davison, attempted to implement constitutional change and improve professionalism, but the symptoms presented did not lead them to a full diagnosis of the disease.[9] This had two separate but related layers of infection, one almost invisibly buried beneath the other. The most visible, which produced malfeasance and misgovernment, was the easiest to treat. The governance and accounting reforms of the 1980s, although only partially complete, may have temporarily alleviated some of the symptoms.[10] While the market continued to grow rapidly, many thought that the patient would make a good recovery. By 1988, however, constitutional reforms alone could not remedy the underlying and most fatal layer of the Lloyd's disease, the toxic process by which risks were insured and reinsured and the unwarranted faith in the competence of those managing that process.

A belief in the traditional ways of doing things compounded the ailment. There were at least two aspects of this. First, tribalism and hierarchical attitudes abounded. Brokers regarded underwriters, some at least, as vain and lazy. Underwriters viewed members' agents as a 'lesser breed'. The staff of Lloyd's were seen by both underwriters and brokers as inferior and 'uncommercial'. All working members regarded the place as special and themselves as superior to those employed by outside insurance companies.[11] Second, these feelings of superiority did not derive from an extensive formal education. As discussed in Chapter 3 above, Lloyd's underwriters rarely had any professional qualifications or a university degree. Many began at Lloyd's as teenage 'entry boys', sitting at the box near the junior and senior underwriters, learning how deals were made with brokers, noting the decisions made on filing cards. If they were reasonably bright, and fitted in well with the lunchtime drinking culture,

[9] Davison later admitted that he, and Fisher before him, in trying to replicate company-type accounting and disclosure rules at Lloyd's, did not appreciate the significance of the long-tail liability problem. Davison, 'Affadavit', 26.

[10] Gwilliam and co-authors find that the benefits, in terms of inducing market expansion, of Lloyd's accounting and auditing reforms of the early 1980s outweighed the costs, but also remark that these reforms could not prevent the later consequences of poor underwriting and monitoring. Gwilliam et. al., 'Costs and Benefits'; *Idem.*, 'Principals and Agents'.

[11] Duguid, *On the Brink*, 18–22.

they would gradually work their way up the seniority system until they became chief underwriter for a syndicate.[12] The sense of superiority came from surviving in this system, being a member of an exclusive club and making lots of money.

An inflated confidence in their own abilities led underwriters into the LMX spiral, a market that many did not understand and whose risks they did not know how to price. During a Council discussion about marine underwriters moving into non-marine lines, such as liability insurance, it was admitted that they 'were ill equipped to assess such risks'.[13] This was not due to a lack of experience. Those who made the massive losses for the Gooda Walker syndicates, for instance, were no Johnny-come-latelies or young Turks seeking to gamble with their Names' funds. Stan Andrews, the underwriter for syndicate #298, was born in 1930, joined the Gooda agency in 1954 and was aged 64 at the time of the GW trial. Anthony Willard, who wrote for syndicate #299, joined Lloyd's aged 16 in 1951 and became marine underwriter for GW in 1968. He was 59 at the time of his trial. Derek Walker was born in 1928, began working in Lloyd's in 1943 and was aged 66 at his trial. In other words, they were all long-established insiders who had worked their way up through the market. Yet it proved hugely damaging for these men to rely on their past experience when writing XL risks that required specialist knowledge and an expert consideration of rating and exposure. Setting premiums by intuition and 'gut feeling' would not do in a world of rapid technological and environmental change, with unprecedented losses from natural catastrophes and long-term liabilities.[14]

Lloyd's not only provides a lesson about the weakness of self-regulation and the inefficiency of the competitive market to weed out poor business practices. It also reveals the damage that can be caused to a complex financial system by dogmatic belief in the competence of experts. The assertion by Lloyd's insiders of their right to self-regulate rested on their expertise and the mysteries of a trade rooted in customary practices. Before the 1980s, this assertion, and widespread ignorance of how Lloyd's operated, had convinced generations of legislators to leave the market alone. But

[12] Davison, *Lloyd's*, 25; Duguid, *On the Brink*, 6–7; Browne, 'Lloyd's', slides 5–6.

[13] Council meeting 7 June 1989, in Lloyd's, *Minutes of Council*, no. 5.

[14] Luessenhop, *Risky Business*, 28; *Deeny v Gooda Walker Ltd.*, 117–18; Berger et. al., 'Reinsurance'.

the claims proved to be a chimera in the face of market forces, climate shocks and changes in the nature of risk.

It is not that doubt was never cast during the period upon the capabilities of those working in Lloyd's. The accounts of the scandals and frauds related in the chapters above provide plenty of evidence of how action groups and their lawyers repeatedly accused underwriters and managing agents of incompetence and failing to protect the interests of Names, and Lloyd's Corporation of incompetence in failing to prevent negligent underwriting or outright fraud.[15] The initial investigation launched into the PCW scandal reported that many of the Lloyd's community in senior positions 'were not even vaguely aware' of the legal obligations on agents to act at all times in the best interests of their principals, not to make secret profits at their principals' expenses, and not to disclose fully all matters affecting their relationship with their principals.[16] At a meeting in 1989, Lloyd's Council itself discussed the 'considerable degree of real irresponsibility' in the market, as revealed by the poor rating of some classes of insurance such as oil rig and construction risks.[17] A Mori poll of 459 Names, commissioned by Lloyd's in 1991, found that 88% were worried about the competence of active underwriters and managing agents, and only slightly fewer were concerned about the competence of members' agents and the ethical standards of underwriters and brokers.[18] James Mackay, a Name on a syndicate caught up in the LMX spiral, described it as an 'incompetence scandal'. Monika Day, a marine underwriter interviewed in 1993, believed that Lloyd's troubles in the 1980s derived from fraud, incompetence and a lack of regulation, and she welcomed the arrival of corporate capital and 'professional risk takers' into the market. Similar views were expressed by figures outside Lloyd's. George Nissen, a former deputy chairman of the London Stock Exchange, interviewed in 1992, thought that the situation at Lloyd's 'all looks extraordinarily amateurish now…', and wondered why the Lloyd's

[15] See Chapter 6, pp. 49, 51, 66; Chapter 7, pp. 79–80; Chapter 8, p. 92.

[16] Letter to Lloyd's Council of 20 January 1984, cited by Justice Cresswell in *Lloyd's v Jaffray*, 289.

[17] Council meeting 1 February 1989, in Lloyd's, *Minutes of Council,* no. 5. The Council were shocked that oil rigs were then being insured at one-tenth of the rates prevailing only a few years earlier, and construction risks in the US at one-third of their former rates.

[18] *Lloyd's Log*, December 1991: 4–5.

community had not been not willing to change: 'Why did they not have clever people who really identified what these problems were?'[19] Mr Justice Cresswell, ruling on the *Lloyd's v Jaffray* trial in 2000, found that 'the catalogue of failings and incompetence in the 1980s by underwriters, managing agents, members' agents, and others….is staggering'. He cited the testimony of the former Lloyd's chairman, Sir David Rowland, that 'competence in areas of the Lloyd's market was seriously lacking in the 1980s', and that 'the level of ability of Lloyd's was not…at the level I would wish…'.[20]

Lloyd's underwriters' claim to expertise rested on their tacit knowledge and their accumulation of know-how.[21] To some outsiders, it was mysterious. To others, it resembled guesswork. Paul Ferris described an encounter when he visited the Room in 1960:

> Suddenly the underwriter said: 'Suppose I quote you a thousand pounds in full for that?' The broker stood upright, help up his hands and smiled: 'Well, I mean, it's anybody's guess'.[22]

As discussed in Chapter 1 above, tacit knowledge is associated with intuition and a reliance on the rule of thumb.[23] This facilitates the decision making required in a fast-moving insurance market like Lloyd's. It also, however, generates systematic biases and errors in predictions, with people assessing risks based on the ease with which instances of the risk event come to mind, and ignoring the effects of random variation in small samples. The problem of the LMX spiral was that the institutional environment at Lloyd's, and the lack of professional education among underwriters, constrained the ability of scientific knowledge and rational analysis to feed into and inform tacit knowledge, and to re-shape business practices.[24]

[19] BL C409/124, interview with James Mackay; C409/121, interview with Monika Day; C409/054, interview with George Nissen.

[20] *Lloyd's v Jaffray*, 298. Rowland was chairman of Lloyd's 1993–97.

[21] On different types of knowledge, see Mokyr, *Gifts of Athena*, Chapter 1.

[22] Ferris, *The City*, 198.

[23] See Chapter 1, p. 4 above.

[24] Mokyr argues that economic and technological development can depend upon the constraints or incentives that institutions impose on different categories of knowledge in any given society. Mokyr, *Gifts of Athena*, 285–97.

Those with experience of Lloyd's in the 1980s observed arrogance and a 'prima donna culture' among the top underwriters.[25] Robert Browne recalled an underwriter from Munich Re, the world's leading major reinsurance company, telling an audience, with only a little exaggeration, that 'we Germans use technical rates. In London they use ceiling rates. The underwriter reads the slip, looks at the ceiling, and puts down the first number which comes into his head'.[26] As modern studies have shown, the success of intuitive decision making depends greatly on the predictability of the environment in which decisions are made.[27] It can deliver profits in the market for staples such as marine and aviation insurance, where risks were usually discrete and well known. However, intuition can also lead underwriters to simplify the decision-making process, rather than basing their assessments of complicated or uncertain risks on fuller information. Intuition may lead them to underinsure against low probability-high loss events or to avoid seeking out additional information when confronted with adverse news—the 'ostrich effect' that has been observed of professional investors.[28] Howard Kunreuther and colleagues have argued that rich context information is necessary for insurers to be able to judge the differences between low probability risks, or to price risks accurately where there is ambiguity about event probability or uncertainty about the scale of possible losses.[29] The information systems and deal making practices employed at Lloyd's did not lend themselves to the acquisition and analysis of such rich contexts.[30]

Many of the findings of the literature on decision making under uncertainty, risk behaviour and the fallacies of experts help explain the behaviour at Lloyd's. A belief in the superiority of their knowledge among

[25] Browne, 'Lloyd's', slide 7.

[26] Browne, 'Lloyd's', slide 6.

[27] Kahneman, *Thinking Fast and Slow*, 201, 240.

[28] Karlsson et. al., 'Ostrich Effect'; Laury et. al., 'Insurance Decisions'.

[29] Kunreuther et. al., 'Ambiguity'; Kunreuther et. al., 'Making Low Probabilities Useful'.

[30] One Council meeting in 1985 was advised that 'there was a need to pay more attention to obtaining information on matters such as the exposure of the (Lloyd's) Market to particular risks'. '…The statistical inevitability of an earthquake on the west coast of the USA (was) one example where such knowledge of exposure would be of benefit. Most insurance companies knew their exposure to such risks'. Council meeting 11 November 1985, in Lloyd's, *Minutes of Council*, no. 2.

underwriters in the LMX spiral, excluding the outright fraudsters, appears to have led to overconfidence and 'cognitive dissonance'—an inability to know the limits of their expertise.[31] Overconfidence, in turn, may have led them to persist in operating according to established beliefs and practices; to 'tunnelling', making inferences too quickly and focusing on a small number of known sources of uncertainty; to 'herding', the desire to avoid being out of line in one's risk assessments with other 'experts' in the market; and to 'confirmation bias', interpreting evidence with the aim of corroborating the rules that underwriters themselves had made up.[32] The practice at Lloyd's of syndicate underwriters 'following' the premium rate set by a recognised 'lead' underwriter would have reinforced these behavioural traits. In his evidence to the GW trial, Richard Outhwaite testified that XL rating was not an exact science, and that most underwriters followed the rate accepted by the leading underwriter on the slip, which in turn was basically what the latter thought the market could bear.[33] This has been called 'cascade pricing', the process by which a lead underwriter, with supposed superior knowledge of the risk, sets the price, and follower underwriters, who sequentially each insure part of the risk, ignore their own risk information signals to follow the price of the lead.[34]

The combined effect of these behaviours on XL underwriting at Lloyd's would have been a heightened tendency to ignore 'black swans', the unknown or unimagined events that can deliver catastrophic losses.[35] There are obvious parallels with the behaviour of investors in the market for sub-prime mortgage default risk whose collapse brought about the global financial crisis of 2007–2008.[36]

[31] Kahneman, *Thinking Fast and Slow*, 218–21, 234–44, 252, 255–7, 263; Syed, *Black Box Thinking*, 109.

[32] See Chapter 1, p. 5 above.

[33] Deeny v Gooda Walker Ltd, 55.

[34] D'Arcy and Oh have shown that this cascade effect can lead to severe bouts of underpricing, as happened in the XL crisis at Lloyd's in the late 1980s. To avoid the danger of a negative cascade, namely rejection of the risk by the lead underwriter being followed by rejections from other underwriters and no insurance being issued, lead underwriters tended to under-price the insurance of large risks such as catastrophe and pollution liabilities. D'Arcy and Oh, 'Cascade Effect'.

[35] Taleb, *Black Swan*.

[36] Gillian Tett, for instance, has questioned the expertise of those involved in the slicing, repackaging and selling of mortgage default risk, a business with similarities to XL

By 1988, no amount of internal governance and accounting reform, no further invasive surgery to the organs of the institution, could have saved Lloyd's from collapse. Fundamental flaws lay buried in market's closed structure and its out-dated practices that proved vulnerable to the cataclysmic losses arising in the 1980s and 1990s. These core weaknesses, however, were nurtured by multiple delusions of competence: the faith of underwriters and brokers in their own know-how; the belief of politicians, successive governments and Lloyd's insiders in the institution's ability to govern and regulate itself; the trust placed by Names and policyholders in Lloyd's and its experts. These external and internal delusions of competence reinforced each other and produced near fatal barriers to change.

reinsurance, in the years before the crisis. Tett, *Fool's Gold*, 113–17, 149, 244. See also O'Neill et. al., 'Coping with the CDS Crisis'.

CHAPTER 10

Epilogue—Lloyd's *Redivivus*

Abstract Before issues arising from the run-off of outstanding liabilities and the impact of corporate membership were fully resolved, Lloyd's suffered further heavy catastrophe losses between 1998 and 2001. Nevertheless, replenished with a growing volume of corporate capital, Lloyd's survived this challenging period and entered a long run of sustained profitability. In 2001, the Financial Services Authority finally became responsible for regulating Lloyd's, reversing the Conservative government's decision of 1986 to preserve self-regulation. More important than external regulation were other drivers of transformation. These were, first, market forces, as well as the impact of climate change, compelling Lloyd's to adopt more scientific methods of risk assessment in order to remain competitive. Second, a new generation of leaders pushed through key institutional reforms that re-envisaged Lloyd's as a franchisor, as a service platform for the insurance industry and as a modern corporate citizen.

Keywords Catastrophe losses · Financial regulation · Risk management · Corporate citizenship · Governance reforms

R. Pearson, *Delusions of Competence*,
Palgrave Studies in Economic History,
https://doi.org/10.1007/978-3-030-94088-1_10

At the spring 1996 meeting of the American Society of Actuaries held in Marco Island, Florida, a session was convened with the title 'Lloyd's of London: does it have a future?'. Many doubted that it did.[1] Much of the discussion centred on two uncertainties: first, the ability of Equitas to manage the run-off of historic liabilities, and of Lloyd's to come to a final agreement with litigating Names; second, the ability of the new 'risk-based capital' calculations, and the information flows required to underpin these, to allow Lloyd's to move forward with a largely corporate membership. Corporate members, their analysts and their investors, it was claimed, had less patience than Lloyd's previous constituency. They wanted to know the assets backing the underwriting and be able to estimate losses and expected returns. Under the old regime of individual Names, no one could accurately quantify the capital behind Lloyd's Central Fund. 'The secret of unlimited liability was not that liability was really unlimited, it was that no one truly knew the assets'.[2]

None of these questions were fully resolved before the Lloyd's market suffered further heavy catastrophe losses between 1998 and 2001, including claims from the 9/11 terrorist attack on New York (see Fig. 8.1). However, supported by an increasing volume of corporate capital, especially from insurance companies based outside the UK, Lloyd's was better placed to recover than it had been in the past. In the years preceding the series of losses at the end of the 1990s, the total underwriting capacity of the Lloyd's market had stagnated at around £10bn. From 2001, capacity began to increase rapidly, reaching £16.1bn by 2007.[3] Lloyd's enjoyed a sustained streak of profitability. There were just two loss-making years (2005 and 2011) between 2002 and 2016. In the five years 2006–2010, the average annual pre-tax return on capital was 22.1%, and the average net result was £3.1bn on a gross premium of £19.1bn. In the five years 2012–2016, the average return was 12.6%, and the average net result was £2.7bn on a gross premium of £26.7bn.[4]

[1] *The Economist* 26 June, 18 September, 13 November 1993, 9 April, 10 December 1994.

[2] James L. Wertheimer, cited in Session 32PD, 'Lloyd's of London', 15. Wertheimer was Vice-President and actuary at UNUM Corporate of Portland, Maine, which was the first insurance company to join Lloyd's as a corporate member.

[3] Calculated from Lloyd's, *Annual Reports* 1994–2007. Cf. also *Sigma* 3 (2002): 14–17.

[4] Calculated from Lloyd's, *Annual Reports* 2002–2018.

In 2001, the Financial Services Authority, the official regulator of the City's financial institutions, finally became responsible for regulating Lloyd's, including monitoring capital levels and solvency. This proved to be no guarantee of the stability and transparency of Lloyd's, not least because the FSA had its own problems of incompetence, as revealed in the financial crisis of 2007–8, when it was criticised for relying too heavily on a 'tick box' approach to regulation.[5] In 2013, the FSA was replaced by the Financial Conduct Authority (FCA).[6] The FCA, however, has also suffered from 'considerable regulatory failings', for instance in its failure to protect bond-holders from the collapse of London Capital & Finance in 2019.[7] External regulation has generally failed to live up to the hopes of those in the 1980s who were calling for it as a panacea for the scandals at Lloyd's and elsewhere.

While not wishing to minimise the importance of external regulatory pressures from UK, EU and overseas governments, the main drivers behind the fundamental transformation of Lloyd's have been market forces and a new generation of leaders pushing through key institutional reforms. Under the chairmanship of Peter Levene from 2002—he remained nine years in office—Lloyd's Corporation re-envisioned itself in three ways: as an institution of market governance, as a service platform for the market and as a modern corporate citizen. In 2002, Levene's strategy group pushed through a reform package in the face of opposition from the Association of Lloyd's Names, who feared that the Council was pandering to the corporate members.[8] The package included the abolition of the traditional three-year system of syndicate accounting and a move to annual accounts. This entailed increasing costs, but it gave Names with

[5] *The Economist* 20 January 2005; H.M. Treasury, *A New Approach*, paragraph 1.3. For an argument that simple and easy-to-communicate methods are more effective than complex information-intensive ones in financial regulation, see Aikman et al., 'Taking Uncertainty Seriously'.

[6] Two new authorities were set up in 2013 and placed under the oversight of the Bank of England: the FCA, which was the conduct watchdog for all regulated financial organisations; and the Prudential Regulatory Authority, which monitored their financial stability.

[7] *Gloster Report*, 293–300.

[8] *The Independent* 18 January 2002; *The Guardian* 18 January 2002; *Financial Times* 18 January 2002. The first business plan was followed by a series of 3-year rolling strategic plans, reviewed on an annual basis, that have continued to the present day. Thus, the plan for 2012–2014 rolled over into the plan for 2013–2015, etc.

unlimited liability an easier means of exiting the market. The admission of new Names on an unlimited liability basis was also ended. By 2014, this category of member accounted for just two per cent of the total underwriting capacity of Lloyd's market.[9] While Lloyd's Council remained the supreme ruling body of the Corporation, a new Franchise Board was introduced to act as an executive that would actively monitor syndicate performance and regulate the underwriting agencies, now to be viewed as Lloyd's 'franchisees'. The Franchise Board included six non-executive directors appointed from outside Lloyd's for their specialist expertise. Thus, the engine of Lloyd's was no longer an unwieldly Council dominated by insiders, but the kind of smaller and more streamlined body of professionals of the type called for by Ian Hay Davison back in the early 1980s.

This re-envisioning of Lloyd's as a 'Franchisor', rather than as a society or a club, was key to its strategy of expanding globally through licensing new vehicles such as 'cover-holders'. Cover-holders were local agents with delegated authority to write insurance on behalf of Lloyd's syndicates, providing local expertise that allowed syndicates to operate in regions or countries as if they were a local insurer. Another vehicle was the 'service company'. These operated like cover-holders, but were wholly owned subsidiaries of a Lloyd's managing agent or its group. Unlike a cover-holder, a service company was able to sub-delegate underwriting authority to other cover-holders. By 2015, there were over 4,000 cover-holders and 242 service companies franchised by Lloyd's, mostly in the UK and North America.[10]

Another aspect of Lloyd's governance transformation was the increasing attention paid to the performance of the Corporation and the security that the market offered to Lloyd's policyholders. Beginning in 2003, annual calculations were made of Lloyd's 'chain of security', namely the assets that backed the insurance policies. The total value of this chain increased from £30bn in 2003 to £80bn by 2017, a higher rate of growth than that of premium volume in the same period.[11] In 2007, Lloyd's began monitoring annually key performance indicators, such as market

[9] Lloyd's, *Annual Report for 2014*, 4.

[10] Lloyd's, *Annual Report for 2015*.

[11] Assets grew by 2.7 fold, compared to 2.2 fold for gross premiums. Calculated from Lloyd's, *Annual Reports*.

performance, solvency deficit, pre-tax return on capital, brand strength, customer and managing agent satisfaction levels, and ratings by the main global rating agencies, Standard & Poor's, Fitch and A.M. Best.

The second dimension of Lloyd's transformation was to re-imagine itself as a service platform to make Lloyd's 'the market of choice' for buyers and sellers of specialist property and casualty insurance and reinsurance.[12] Over the years since 2002, a wide range of services have been developed, focusing on business processes such as policy management and claims handling, on performance management and, above all, on risk management. Lloyd's introduced a standard 'London Market Principles' insurance slip in 2004 to promote 'contract certainty' for its policyholders. A 'Claims Change Programme' was launched in 2008 to improve claims handling processes. Within four years, this was delivering 49% reduction in transaction times for the 45,000 claims in the programme.[13] A Risk Committee was established in 2006 to monitor and assess overall risks in the market. A '360 Risk Project' was introduced in 2007 to generate a programme of research and analysis on three areas: climate change, political violence and terrorism, and corporate liability. A new metric, the Individual Capital Assessment, was designed in the same year, to measure the level of capital resources required to withstand a 1-in-200 year event over a three-year time frame, as part of stress and scenario testing for each type of risk.[14] An Emerging Risks Team was tasked to identify new types of risk and changes to existing hazards, such as the impact of climate change on flood risk. The team produced a number of innovative research reports, for example on nanotechnology (2007), pandemics (2008), synthetic biology (2009) and solar storm risk to the North American electric grid (2013). A Catastrophe Response Team was set up in 2011, and two years later, a new online tool, 'On the Ground Global Profiles', was launched to help Lloyd's managing agents deal with local claims after a large catastrophe loss.[15]

This intensive sustained focus on risk analysis and management marked a catching up by Lloyd's with developments that had begun years earlier

[12] Lloyd's, *Annual Report for 2008*, 18.

[13] Lloyd's, *Annual Report for 2008*, 41; *Annual Report for 2012*, 18.

[14] Lloyd's, *Annual Report for 2007*, 41.

[15] Lloyd's, *Annual Report for 2011*, 5; *Annual Report for 2013*, 16.

in the company sector.[16] It was a world away from the days when some Lloyd's underwriters failed to understand or bothered to estimate catastrophe risks, and were under no pressure from the Corporation to do so.[17] It also reflected a new outward-facing Lloyd's as it moved towards closer cooperation with the rest of the London market and the global insurance industry. In May 2012, Lloyd's Vision 2025 was launched by British Prime Minister David Cameron at an event in the Lloyd's building. Vision 2025 was 'designed to ensure that Lloyd's remains the global hub for specialist insurance and reinsurance', by growing premium income around the world and by establishing a small number of overseas hubs in markets such as India, Mexico, Brazil, China and Singapore.[18]

A third element in Lloyd's transformation was its greater attention to the brand, to its responsibilities to the community at large and to its own employees. The corporation's activities and publications reveal a desire to be a good corporate citizen that was more professional, more transparent and more aware of issues such as diversity, inclusiveness, gender inequality and environmental sustainability than had ever been the case before. Lloyd's Community Programme, which focused on the education of young people in East London, had commenced in 1989 with a few hundred volunteers drawn from Lloyd's market, By 2018, it was supported by over 50 companies and over 3,000 volunteers. Lloyd's Charities Trust also greatly diversified its activities. Regular surveys were conducted to measure the satisfaction levels of policyholders, brokers, underwriters, cover-holders and the opinions of Lloyd's employees. The number of Corporation employees, which had sunk to a low of 582 in 2003, largely as a result of computerisation, grew again to over 1,000 by 2018 as the volume of Lloyd's business increased.[19] Lloyd's set out

[16] On Swiss Re's new company-wide integrated risk management system of the 1990s, see Straumann, 'The Invisible Giant', 341–4. For surveys of developments since the 1980s in catastrophe modelling and catastrophe reinsurance, see Cutler and Zechhauser, 'Reinsurance for Catastrophes'; Lechner et al., 'Continuity and Change'.

[17] See above Chapter 7, pp. 80–2 and Chapter 9, p. 110.

[18] Lloyd's, *Annual Report for 2011*, 4; *Annual Report for 2012*, 1, 17. It should be noted, however, that most of Lloyd's premium growth between 2004 and 2018 occurred in North America. The latter accounted for 34% of business in 2004, and 51% in 2018. The UK and Europe together declined from 42% to 27% in the same period.

[19] Total employment was around 2,000 from the 1970s to the late 1990s. The impact of the computerization of functions and the rapid decline in staffing numbers resulted in enormous labour productivity gains at Lloyd's. In 1990, net premiums per Corporation

to become an 'Employer of Choice' by investing in employee welfare, engagement and career development. After an 11-year hiatus, Lloyd's re-entered the graduate market in 2007 with a new recruitment campaign. The Corporation also began attending campus fairs and making presentations to career advisors from top-tier universities.[20] For the first time, Lloyd's earned a place in *The Times Top 100 Graduate Employers*.[21] In 2006, a 'Lloyd's Developing Leaders Programme' was launched in cooperation with the London Business School to improve leadership skills. Internships, mentoring and talent review schemes were launched. In 2013, Lloyd's established its first apprenticeship programme for school leavers.

This fundamental transformation of Lloyd's as a corporate citizen, as a governance structure and as a service 'platform' or 'commercial partner' for the global insurance and reinsurance industry modernised Lloyd's. It wiped away the opaque practices and stuffy upper-class white male hierarchies of old. In 2014, Lloyd's appointed Inga Beale as its first female chief executive. In 2016, Hilary Weaver was appointed the Corporation's chief risk officer. The greater diversity and professionalism of senior management, the rising quality of the talent pool, the new transparent and scientific approach to business processes and risk management together can never guarantee absolutely the end to delusions of competence at Lloyd's, but they do significantly limit the scope for incompetence to fester unnoticed, with the kind of devastating consequences that were witnessed at the end of the twentieth century.

employee were £2.5m. By 2003, the figure was £14.6m (in constant 1990 £), and in 2018 £10.8m. Calculated from Lloyd's, *Annual Reports*.

[20] Lloyd's, *Annual Report for 2007*, 42.

[21] Lloyd's, *Annual Report for 2010*, 33.

Glossary

Coverholder: A local agent—an individual or company, often outside the UK, with delegated authority to write insurance on behalf of a Lloyd's syndicate.

Errors and Omissions insurance: A form of liability insurance taken out by Lloyd's members' agents and managing agents to indemnify themselves against negligence claims made by members of their syndicates.

Long-tail: A term that describes classes of insurance where settlement of claims may not take place until many years after the issue of the policies.

Managing Agent: The underwriting agent (normally a limited company or partnership) that has the day-to-day conduct of a syndicate or group of syndicates on behalf of all Names who are members of these syndicates.

Members' Agent: An agent (normally a limited company or partnership) that advises Names on their choice of syndicates, places Names on the syndicates of their choice and provides general advice to Names regarding the underwriting done on their behalf.

Name: A member of a Lloyd's syndicate, who is either the active underwriter for that syndicate, or who invests in the syndicate 'passively' (like a 'sleeping partner'), in order for the underwriter to write insurance on his/her behalf.

R. Pearson, *Delusions of Competence*,
Palgrave Studies in Economic History,
https://doi.org/10.1007/978-3-030-94088-1

Reinsurance: The insurance of insurers, where a first or direct insurer underwrites a risk and then 'cedes' or reinsures (or 'lays-off' in bookmakers' parlance) part of that risk to another insurer (the reinsurer) for the payment of a premium. There is no contractual relationship between the reinsurer and the original insured. The responsibility of the first insurer to the policyholder for the full amount insured is not affected by any reinsurance.

Excess of loss reinsurance: A reinsurance contract between the first or direct insurer of a risk and the reinsurer, where the reinsurer's liability commences above a given sum on an individual loss.

Quota share reinsurance: A reinsurance contract where a given proportion of the whole risk insured by the first insurer is reinsured.

Stop loss reinsurance: A reinsurance contract where the first insurer is reinsured for any loss above a given sum.

Reinsurance to close: A reinsurance policy purchased by an underwriter that would pay for any outstanding or future claims that occurred after the end of a syndicate's term and the closure of its three-year account.

Run-off: A run-off contract is a contract by which a syndicate or an insurance company is reinsured against outstanding and potential future liabilities, claims and expenses in respect of business written in past years of account as specified in the contract.

Time and distance reinsurance: A reinsurance contract where the pay-out under the contract cannot be made until a given period of time has elapsed after the contract is agreed, and where the amount of indemnity available is determined by the investment earnings on the original premium over that period of time.

Rollover policies: Insurance or reinsurance policies that were agreed to be 'rolled over' into a new term, without the issue of a new policy.

Retrocession: The insurance of reinsurers, namely where a reinsurer reinsures a risk and then 'retrocedes' part of that risk to another insurer (the retrocessionary) for the payment of a premium.

Syndicate: A group of individuals underwriting insurance through the common agency of a managing agent, each of whom put up his/her personal assets as a backing, and take a proportion of the insurance for himself/herself, with unlimited liability for his/her proportion of the risk insured.

Bibliography

Primary Sources

British Library:

Sound recordings—National Life Stories: City Lives. Interviews with Sir Peter Miller, C409/015; Dennis Presland, C409/020; Leonard Toomey, C409/026; Terence Higgins, C409/027; Gwilym H. Lewis, C409/033; George Nissen, C409/054; Francis Holford, C409/067; Monika Day, C409/121; C409/124, James Mackay.

London Metropolitan Archive:

Lloyd's of London, *Minutes of the General Meeting of Members, 1976–81*, CLC/B/ 148/A/006/Ms31570/012.

Lloyd's of London, *Minutes of Meetings of the Committee of Lloyd's*, no.109, 1985, CLC/B/148/A/001/Ms31571/146.

Lloyd's of London, *Minutes of Council, no.1, 1983–4*, CLC/B/148/A/005/ Ms38565/001.

Lloyd's of London, *Minutes of Council, no.2, 1985–6,* CLC/B/148/A/005/ Ms38565/002.

Lloyd's of London, *Minutes of Council, no.3, 1987*, CLC/B/148/A/005/ Ms38565/003.

Lloyd's of London, *Minutes of Council, no.4, 1988*, CLC/B/148/A/005/ Ms38565/004.

Lloyd's of London, *Minutes of Council, no.5, 1989*, CLC/B/148/A/005/ Ms38565/005.

R. Pearson, *Delusions of Competence*, Palgrave Studies in Economic History, https://doi.org/10.1007/978-3-030-94088-1

Lloyd's of London, *Annual Reports* 1974–80, 1994–2018.

National Archives, London:

PREM 19/1601, Prime Minister's visit to Lloyd's, 1 February 1985.

T364/506, Lloyd's 1985.

T364/509, Lloyd's 1987.

T450/349, Lloyd's Insurance/Treasury relations 1983 to 1985.

Law Reports:

Deeny v Gooda Walker Ltd, before the Hon. Mr Justice Phillips, Commercial Court, Queens Bench Division, Royal Courts of Justice, 4 October 1994.

Society of Lloyd's of London v Sir William Jaffray and others, before Hon. Mr Justice Cresswell, Commercial Court, Queen's Bench Division, Royal Courts of Justice, 3 November 2000.

Society of Lloyd's v John Trevor Howard Henderson and Others, before Justice Andrew Smith, Commercial Court, Queen's Bench Division Royal Courts of Justice, 11 May 2005, (2005) All ER (D) 155 (May).

Ian Hay Davison, 'Affadavit of Ian Hay Davison, 4 March 2005', *Society of Lloyd's v Henderson*, Commercial Court, Queen's Bench Division, 1996 Folio no. 2032., reproduced in www.TruthAboutLloyds.com.

British Parliamentary Papers

House of Commons Debates (Hansard) 1976–86.

House of Lords Debates (Hansard) 1981–6.

Report of the Committee to Review the Functioning of Financial Institutions (Wilson Committee), command 7937 (June 1980).

Treasury and Civil Service Committee, *Fifth Special Report—Financial Services Regulation: Self-Regulation at Lloyd's of London: The Government's Response to the Fifth Report from the Committee in Session 1994–95*, command 745 (18 July 1995).

Newspapers and Periodicals

The Economist

Financial Times

The Guardian

The Independent

Lloyd's Log

The Review

Sigma

The Times

Secondary Literature

Daron Acemoglu, Munther A. Dahleh, Ilan Lobel and Asuman Ozdaglar, 'Bayesian Learning in Social Networks'. *The Review of Economic Studies* 78 (2011): 1201–36.

David Aikman, Mirta Galesic, Gerd Gigenrenzer, Sujit Kapadia, and Konstantonous Katiskopoulos, 'Taking Uncertainty Seriously: Simplicity Versus Complexity in Financial Regulation', *Industrial and Corporate Change* 30 (2021): 317–45.

Erik Angner, 'Economists as Experts: Overconfidence in Theory and Practice', *Journal of Economic Methodology* 13 (2006): 1–24.

Masahiro Ashiya and Takero Doi, 'Herd Behavior of Japanese Economists', *Journal of Economic Behavior & Organization* 46 (2001): 343–6.

Andrew Bain, 'Insurance Spirals and the Lloyd's Market', University of Glasgow, Department of Economics Working Paper, n.d.

Tom Baker, 'Uncertainty > Risk: Lessons for Legal Thought from the Insurance Runoff Market', *Boston College Law Review* 62 (2021): 59–108.

Abhijit V. Banerjee, 'A Simple Model of Herd Behavior', *Quarterly Journal of Economics* 107 (1992): 797–817.

Peter W. J. Bartrip, '"Enveloped in Fog": The Asbestos Problem in Britain's Royal Naval Dockyards, 1949–1999', *International Journal of Maritime History* 26 (2014): 685–701.

Pietro Battiston, Ridhi Kashyap and Valentina Rotondi, 'Reliance on Scientists and Experts During an Epidemic: Evidence from the COVID-19 Outbreak in Italy', *SSM—Population Health* 13 (2021), online. https://doi.org/10.1016/j.ssmph.2020.100721.

Richard Beard, *Sad Little Men: Private Schools and the Ruin of England* (London, 2021).

Jeremy Bentham, *Rationale of Judicial Evidence* (London, 1827).

Nathan Berg and Donald Lein, 'Does Society benefit from Investor Overconfidence in the Ability of Financial Market Experts?', *Journal of Economic Behavior & Organization* 58 (2005): 95-116.

Lawrence Berger, J. David Cummins and Sharon Tennyson, 'Reinsurance and the Liability Insurance Crisis', *Journal of Risk and Uncertainty* 5 (1992): 253–72.

Ronald Bewley and Denzil G. Fiebig, 'On the Herding of Interest Rate Forecasters', *Empirical Economics* 27 (2002): 403–25.

Eugenio F. Biagini, 'Liberalism and Direct Democracy: John Stuart Mill and the Model of Ancient Athens', in Eugenio F. Biagini ed., *Citizenship and Community: Liberals, Radicals and Collective Identities in the British Isles, 1865–1931* (Cambridge, 1996), pp. 21–44.

Sushil Bikhchandani, David Hirschleifer and Ivo Welch, 'Learning from the Behavior of Others: Conformity, Fads, and Informational Cascades', *Journal of Economic Perspectives* 12 (1998): 151–70.

Anthony Brown, *Hazard Unlimited: The Story of Lloyd's of London* (London, 1973).

Anthony Brown, *Cuthbert Heath, Maker of the Modern Lloyd's of London* (Newton Abbot, 1980).

Robert Woodthorpe Browne, 'Lloyd's: The McDonald's of the Insurance Industry', Unpublished paper presented at Gresham College, Barnard's Inn Hall, London, 3 February 2010.

Per L. Bylund and Mark D. Packard, 'Separation of Power and Expertise: Evidence of the Tyranny of Experts in Sweden's COVID-19 Responses', *Southern Economic Journal* 87 (2021): 1300–19.

S. D. Chapman, 'Hogg Robinson: The Rise of a Lloyd's Broker', in Oliver M. Westall ed., *The Historian and the Business of Insurance* (Manchester, 1984), pp. 173–89.

Caroline A. Clarke and David Knights, 'Practice makes Perfect? Skilful Performances in Veterinary Work', *Human Relations* 71 (2018): 1395–1421.

Hugh Cockerell, 'Lloyd's of London', in Adele Hast ed., *International Directory of Company Histories*, vol. III. (Chicago and London, 1991).

Janet Currie and W. Bentley Macleod, 'Diagnosing Expertise: Human Capital, Decision Making, and Performance among Physicians', *Journal of Labor Economics* 35 (2017): 1–43.

David M. Cutler and Richard J. Zeckhauser, 'Reinsurance for Catastrophes and Cataclysms', in Kenneth A. Froot ed., *The Financing of Catastrophe Risk* (Chicago, 1999), pp. 233–74.

Bernard John Daenzer, 'The Non-Admitted Market Abroad', *Journal of Risk and Insurance* 33 (1966): 33–42.

Stephen P. D'Arcy and Pyungsuk Oh, 'The Cascade Effect in Insurance Pricing', *Journal of Risk and Insurance* 64 (1997): 465–80.

Ian Hay Davison, *Lloyd's: Change and Disclosure: A View of the Room* (London, 1987).

Richard Deaves, Erik Lüders and Michael Schröder, 'The Dynamics of Overconfidence: Evidence from Stock Exchange Forecaster', *Journal of Economic Behavior & Organization* 75 (2010): 402–12.

Françoise Delamare Le Deist and Jonathan Winterton, 'What is Competence?' *Human Resource Development International* 8 (2005): 27–46.

Roberta Dessi and Xiaojian Zhao, 'Overconfidence, Stability and Investments', *Journal of Economic Behavior & Organization* 145 (2018): 474–94.

Ian Dilks, 'London Market Sees Evolutionary Changes Beyond Lloyd's Renaissance', *National Underwriter/Property & Casualty Risk & Benefits Management* 101 (9 January 1997).

Andrew Duguid, *On the Brink: How a Crisis Transformed Lloyd's of London* (London, 2014).

David Dunning, Kerri Johnson, Joyce Ehrlinger and Justin Kruger, 'Why People Fail to Recognize Their Own Incompetence', *Current Directions in Psychological Science* 12 (2003): 83–7.

Gerlinde Fellner, Werner Güth and Boris Maciejovsky, 'Illusion of Expertise in Portfolio Decisions: An Experimental Approach', *Journal of Economic Behavior & Organization* 55 (2004): 355–76.

Paul Ferris, *The City* (Harmondsworth, 1965).

Joseph A. Fields, Linda S. Klein and Edward G. Myskowski, 'Lloyd's Financial Distress and Contagion with the US Property and Liability Insurance Industry', *Journal of Risk and Uncertainty* 16 (1998): 173–85.

Matthew Fisher and Frank C. Keil, 'The Curse of Expertise: When More Knowledge leads to Miscalibrated Explanatory Insight', *Cognitive Science* 40 (2016): 1251–69.

Brandon L. Garrett and Gregory Mitchell, 'The Proficiency of Experts', *University of Pennsylvania Law Review* 166 (2018): 901–60.

Malcolm Gladwell, *The Tipping Point: How Little Things Can Make a Big Difference* (London, 2001).

Rt Hon Dame Elizabeth Gloster, DBE, *Report of the Independent Investigation in the Financial Conduct Authority's Regulation of London Capital & Finance plc* (*Gloster Report*) (London: HMSO, 23 November 2020, revised 10 December 2020).

Sarah Goddard, 'Lloyd's Profit, R&R Plan End Market's Dark Days', *Business Insurance* 31 (22 December 1997).

Cathy Gunn, *Nightmare on Lime Street: Whatever Happened to Lloyd's of London?* (London, 1993).

D. Gwilliam, R. Macve and G. Meeks, 'Principals and Agents in Crisis: Reforms of Accounting and Audit at Lloyd's, 1982–6', *Accounting History* 5 (2000): 61–91.

D. Gwilliam, R. Macve and G. Meeks, 'The Costs and Benefits of Increased Accounting Regulation: A Case Study of Lloyd's of London', *Accounting and Business Research* 35 (2005): 129–46.

Diana B. Henriques, *Bernie Madoff: The Wizard of Lies* (New York, 2011).

John D. Hey, Gianna Lotito and Anna Maffioletti, "The Descriptive and Predictive Adequacy of Theories of Decision Making Under Uncertainty/Ambiguity', *Journal of Risk and Uncertainty* 41 (2010): 81–111.

Her Majesty's Treasury, *A New Approach to Financial Regulation: Summary of Consultation Responses* (London: H.M. Treasury, 2010).

Godfrey Hodgson, *Lloyd's of London: A Reputation at Risk* (London, 1986).

Paula Jarzabkowski, Rebecca Bednarek and Paul Spee, *Making a Market for Acts of God: The Practice of Risk Trading in the Global Reinsurance Industry* (Oxford, 2015).

Daniel Kahneman, *Thinking Fast and Slow* (London, 2011).

Sanghoon Hoonie Kang and Jerry Kim, 'The Fragility of Experts: A Moderated-Mediation Model of Expertise, Expert Identity Threat, and Overprecision', *Academy of Management Journal* (2021), online. https://doi.org/10.5465/amj.2019.0899.

Niklas Karlsson, George Loewenstein and Duane Seppi, 'The Ostrich Effect: Selective Attention to Information', *Journal of Risk and Uncertainty* 38 (2009): 95–115.

Bryan Kellett, 'Regulation or Strangulation', *Lloyd's Log* (February 1985): 4–6.

Christopher Kingston, 'Marine Insurance in Britain and America, 1720–1844: A Comparative Institutional Analysis', *Journal of Economic History* 67 (2007): 379–409.

Howard Kunreuther, Jacqueline Meszaros, Robin M. Hogarth and Mark Spranca, 'Ambiguity and Underwriter Decision Processes', *Journal of Economic Behaviour and Organization* 26 (1995): 337–52.

Howard Kunreuther, Nathan Novemsky and Daniel Kahneman, 'Making Low Probabilities Useful', *Journal of Risk and Uncertainty* 23 (2001): 102–20.

Susan K. Laury, Melayne Morgan McInnes and J. Todd Swarthout, 'Insurance Decisions for Low-Probability Losses', *Journal of Risk and Uncertainty* 39 (2009): 17–44.

Roman Lechner, Niels Viggo Haeuter and Lawrence Kenny, 'Continuity and Change in Reinsurance 1990–2016', in Niels Viggo Haeuter and Geoffrey Jones eds., *Managing Risk in Reinsurance: From City Fires to Global Warming* (Oxford, 2017), pp. 277–300.

Moa Lidén and Itiel E. Dror, 'Expert Reliability in Legal Proceedings: "Eeny, Meeny, Miny, Moe, with Which Expert Should We Go?"', *Science & Justice* 61 (2021): 37–46.

Lloyd's of London, *Self-Regulation at Lloyd's: Report of the Fisher Working Party* (London, 1980).

Lloyd's of London, *Regulatory Arrangements at Lloyd's: Report of the Committee of Enquiry (Neill Report)* (London, 1987).

Lloyd's of London, *Report of an Inquiry into Lloyd's Syndicate Participations and the LMX Spiral (Walker Report)* (London, 1992).

Elizabeth Luessenhop, *Risky Business: An Insider's Account of the Disaster at Lloyd's of London* (New York, 1995).

Ulrike Malmendier and Geoffrey Tate, 'CEO Overconfidence and Corporate Investment', *Journal of Finance* 60 (2005): 2661–2700.

Jonathan Mantle, *For Whom the Bell Tolls: Lessons of Lloyd's of London* (London, 1992).

Lee Moerman, Sandra van der Laan and David Campbell, "A Tale of Two Asbestos Giants: Corporate Reports as (Auto)biography," *Business History* 56 (2014): 985–6.
Joel Mokyr, *The Gifts of Athena: Historical Origins of the Knowledge Economy* (Princeton, 2002).
William C. O'Neill, Nilam R. Sharma, Michael T. Carolan and Zainab Charchafchi, 'Coping with the CDS Crisis: Lessons Learned from the LMX Spiral', *Journal of Reinsurance* 16 (2009): 1–34.
Brian O'Shea and Michiko Ueda, 'Who Is More Likely to Ignore Experts' Advice Related to COVID-19?', *Preventive Medicine Reports* 23 (2021), online. https://doi.org/10.1016/j.pmedr.2021.101470.
Robin Pearson, 'Cuthbert Eden Heath (1859–1939)', in Colin Matthew ed., *The Oxford Dictionary of National Biography* (Oxford, 2004).
Robin Pearson, 'Lloyd's of London', in John J. McCusker ed., *History of World Trade Since 1450* (Farmington Hills, MI, 2006), Vol. 2, pp. 466–9.
Robin Pearson, 'United Kingdom: Pioneering Insurance Internationally', in Peter Borscheid and Niels Viggo Haueter eds., *World Insurance: The Evolution of a Global Risk Network* (Oxford, 2012), pp. 67–97.
Robin Pearson and Mikael Lönnborg, 'Naturkatastrofer och Försäkringsbolag på Främmande Marknader', *Nordisk Försäkringstidskrift* 86 (2005): 77–91.
Patrick Proctor, *For Whom the Bell Tolls* (Harlow, 1996).
Adam Raphael, *Ultimate Risk: The Inside Story of the Lloyd's Catastrophe* (New York, 1995).
Harold E. Raynes, *A History of British Insurance* (London, 1964).
H. Rice and M. G. White, 'Reinsurance to Close at Lloyd's and Related Issues', Unpublished paper, GISG Convention, October 1990.
Tilmann J. Röder, *Rechtsbildung im Wirtschaftlichen "Weltverkehr". Das Erdbeben von San Francisco und die Internationale Standardisierung von Vertragsbedingungen (1871–1914)* (Frankfurt am Main, 2006).
Session 32PD, 'Lloyd's of London: Does It Have a Future?', *Record: Proceedings of the Society of Actuaries* 22 (1996): 1–25.
Richard Brinsley Sheridan, *The School for Scandal: A Comedy* (1777, Project Gutenberg ebook, www.gutenberg.org).
Daniel Simpson, 'The Unhealthy History of Asbestos', *Lloyd's Log*, December 1991: 24–6.
John Southerst, 'Unnatural Disasters', *Canadian Business* 65 (1992): 83–100.
Jeffrey W. Stempel, 'Assessing the Coverage Carnage: Asbestos Liability and Insurance After Three Decades of Dispute', *Connecticut Insurance Law Journal* 12 (2005–6): 349–476.
Tobias Straumann, 'The Invisible Giant: The Story of Swiss Re 1863–2013', in Harold James ed., *The Value of Risk: Swiss Re and the History of Reinsurance* (Oxford, 2013), pp. 237–352.

Matthew Syed, *Black Box Thinking: Marginal Gains and the Secret of High Performance* (London, 2015).

Nassim Nicholas Taleb, *The Black Swan: The Impact of the Highly Improbable* (London, 2007).

Gillian Tett, *Fool's Gold* (London, 2009).

Nuria Tolsá-Caballero and Chia-Jung Tsay, 'Blinded by our Sight: Understanding the Prominence of Visual Information in Judgements of Competence and Performance', *Current Opinion in Psychology* (2021), online. https://doi.org/10.1016/j.copsyc.2021.07.003.

Clive Trebilcock, *Phoenix Assurance and the Development of British Insurance, Volume 2, 1870–1984: The Era of the Insurance Giants* (Cambridge, 1998).

Geoffrey Tweedale, *Magic Mineral to Killer Dust: Turner & Newall and the Asbestos Hazard* (Oxford, 2000).

Geoffrey Tweedale and David Jeremy, 'Compensating the Workers: Industrial Injury and Compensation in the British Asbestos Industry, 1930s–60s', *Business History* 41 (1999): 102–20.

Robert Verkaik, *Posh Boys: How English Public Schools Ruin Britain* (London, 2018).

W. Kip Viscusi, 'Alternative Institutional Responses to Asbestos', *Journal of Risk and Uncertainty* 12 (1996): 147–70.

Richard Webb, 'Enough of Experts? Interview with Roger Kneebone', *New Scientist* 249, 2 June 2021, no. 3320: 40–3.

Welf Werner, 'Hurricane Betsy and the Malfunctioning of the London Reinsurance Market: An Analysis of Transatlantic Reinsurance Trade, 1949–89', *Financial History Review* 14 (2007): 7–28.

Sarah Wilson, *The Origins of Modern Financial Crime: Visible Lessons from Invisible Crimes* (London, 2014).

Charles Wright and C. Ernest Fayle, *A History of Lloyd's* (London, 1928).

Ting Zhang, Kelly B. Harrington and Elad N. Sherf, 'The Errors of Experts: When Expertise Hinders Effective Provision and Seeking of Advice and Feedback', *Current Opinion in Psychology* (2021), online. https://doi.org/10.1016/j.copsyc.2021.06.011.

Paul Zinkewicz, 'London—The Environment Has Changed', *Insurance Advocate* 108 (25 October 1997).

Index

R. Pearson, *Delusions of Competence*,
Palgrave Studies in Economic History,
https://doi.org/10.1007/978-3-030-94088-1

Printed in the USA
CPSIA information can be obtained
at www.ICGtesting.com
LVHW012016181223
766719LV00006B/508

9 783030 940874